Make the

Juice

worth the

Squeeze!

Short and Sweet Solutions
for Managing
Sticky Problems at Work

The MROI team

*For dear Berit,
Someone who gets the
juice out of life!*

Published by MROI

Published by MROI 2008

Typeset in Arial

Printed on Vancouver Opaque PEFC-certified paper
(Pan-European Forest Certification is a system that takes into
account the environmental aspects of forestry)

PEFC

ISBN 978 0 9559179 0 5

Designed by www.comms-plus.co.uk

Printed in Great Britain by Biddles Ltd, King's Lynn, Norfolk

Praise for this book

"Real leaders already practice all the concepts in this book. Now those who wish to realise their full potential and reach for excellence have a manual that shows them how to achieve these objectives, and which brings together a brilliant blend of expertise in dealing with everyday management headaches. Great leaders would do well to follow the MROI recipe for success!"
Neil Sachdev, Commercial Director, Sainsburys

"A refreshing pool of wisdom for leaders to take regular dips into."
Penny de Valk, CEO Institute of Leadership and Management

"It is not often, in this busy world we live in today, to find a business book that you simply cannot put down, with every chapter reminding us, as leaders, of the common sense we need to apply to our roles. 'Make the Juice worth the Squeeze!' is such a book. As I read through the book I experienced many 'aha' moments as I recalled situations where I did a good job and many where I was less than good – I simply forgot the basics. I describe this book as a back to basics 'ready reckoner', a book all leaders should have close at hand, a book they can refer to from time to time when something is not working or when a way forward is being sought. The MROI Team has hit on a winner here."
Robert S Drew, former Chief Executive, Vistage Int. – the largest chief executive membership in the world

"A refreshingly simple handbook for the business leaders of today. These tried-and-tested theories, tools and techniques are essential to develop leadership capability and aid business decision-making."
Pinky Lilani OBE, creator of The Asian Women of Achievement awards, The Women of the Future awards and many other inspirational initiatives

Acknowledgements

Thank you to clients, colleagues and all our friends in the business community who've contributed to and inspired our work since 1993. Here's to the future!

What's on the menu

Essential tools to develop leadership capability
and aid business decision-making

Introduction: A fresh approach

How can Results be measured in the context of developing people within an organisation? How can Value be assessed in leadership development? How can the Quality of an individual's or team's growth be appraised? Such questions about what many consider the soft skills of business, often receive subjective answers. Consequently, the merits of investment in development remain vague. Few people know how to assess the difference between a good and a mediocre return. Is it possible to establish a hard measure on the soft stuff? How can the return on investment (ROI) be ensured? Which fruits are worth squeezing?

Throughout my career in retail, commercial and operational management, there were many times when investing in management training and development programmes produced a lack of return. Something was missing. There seemed to be no structure for understanding the relationship between the contribution of individuals and teams, and the achievement of business objectives. This question of measurement led me to build a new way of working with client organisations: a way that breaks the mental paradigm of consultants being an expensive resource; a way that focuses on leadership contribution as a power for good; a way that creates and guarantees ROI. That's our promise.

HOW it all Started

Back in 1993, I started my own company to manage the development of individuals and teams within organisations. Our mission is to accelerate success in business and inspire future generations of leadership contribution. I believe that commercial organisations have the most powerful presence in this world: way beyond countries; way beyond governments. Leaders have the opportunity to choose how they want to use that power – for themselves, for the organisation and for the world. Perhaps their greatest contribution is not what is usually recognised: not the bottom line, profit and loss, not the financial return shareholders will make. These all matter, but also what's beyond that.

The role each leader occupies in reality is only a very temporary stewardship. Future leaders will inherit the fruits of their decisions. So how they choose to wield their power during their time of office becomes the legacy of their contribution. What excites me is how our work can support the positive impact leaders can make through using this power wisely. Whether we work with coaching individuals specifically, or facilitating groups and teams, or assisting commercial relationships within and between organisations, we maintain a firm focus on the overall desired results from increasing leadership contribution: The Return On Investment.

Our approach aims to satisfy three different requirements:

1. Meaningful principles
2. Measurable process
3. Methods that work

MEANINGFUL Principles

The principle that drives our operation is based on our intention to deliver results for the highest possible motive. Our core purpose is to co-ordinate our collective range of abilities to support the individual, the team and the organisation. No one consultant is complete, just as no role model or mentor can ever be complete. We've seen there is a huge benefit in tapping into the expertise, knowledge and perspectives of different consultants who work together as a team towards the objective of increasing results for the organisation.

MEASURABLE Process

Absolute truth and integrity are our highest measure. We build
a three-way relationship between the individual / team, the
business sponsor and ourselves. When in this relationship,
we drive for openness and honesty so that we are dealing with
reality rather than concept. Any change needs to be set in
current reality. Anything conceptual is wishful or theoretical.
Reality may be tough sometimes, but with truth, it's easier to
progress and it's easier to measure.

Why our measurement process is different to, and has more
truth than, the traditional feedback measures is because of
our focus on qualitative rather than quantitative measurement.
Context and individual makeup become variables in the
measurement process. We assess the need, define the
deliverables, and then measure progress and success against
a set of business based KPIs, that we have agreed with the
individual client team and business sponsor. Required results
have been identified by the business sponsor and progress
against them is measured by that sponsor.

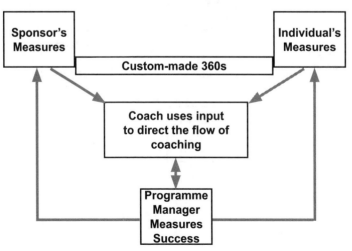

METHODS That Work

Rather than delivering 'off the peg' packages, each consultant on the team draws on their own depth of expertise, their own unique blend of techniques and skills to provide unique support for each solution. We do not subscribe to any particular model, concept or tool. No model is a panacea. Our preference is to simply use models, concepts and tools as a way of helping our clients make sense of their reality and, in turn, create future direction. In this way we are catalysts not programme deliverers.

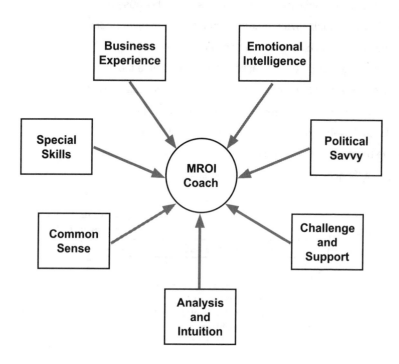

Through grace, grit and good luck, I've been blessed with talented, loyal and trustworthy consultants who have helped to build the success and reputation of our company. Between us we've totted up hundreds of thousands of hours of experience, working with not only top blue chip companies, but also medium and small businesses both in the UK and across the globe. Noticing the consistency of our successful results over the years, and receiving accolades of positive feedback from our clients, it made sense to name our company 'MROI' and confidently trade on our promise: to create Maximum, Meaningful, Measurable 'ROI' (Return on Investment).

WHY We Wrote This Book

There was a gap in the market for a handbook that could support leaders facing their daily 'people' challenges. When working with clients in person, such backup reference material could double the effectiveness of the changes being made. So, thinking about some of the most typical 'people' problems that come up in business, we decided to share some of our experience, how we would approach such problems with some of the common tools we use. Our clients have found these tools to be extremely effective.

We decided to work together as a team to write this book in order to share some of what's worked so well for us. Since we often combine our skills and draw from each other's fields of expertise and diverse backgrounds in order to create the best results for each client, we know from experience that having different perspectives is a real attribute.

We share the belief that healthy organisations can play a powerful, positive role in the world. That our work can help build more successful leaders in business, and more creative and productive teams. That through supporting the growth and achievement of business objectives in this way, we will support the greater contribution that those leaders and organisations can make across the globe.

If you'd like to know more about how coaching could help your organisation, we hope that this book provides some answers. Enjoy!

Maggie Rose *Founder of MROI www.mroi.co.uk*

PREFACE: Recipes That Work

What This Book Offers You

'Is The Juice Worth The Squeeze?' When one of our clients first used these words, we all laughed! It so succinctly summed up the simple truth of decisions that leaders are continually making. Is the anticipated output worth the effort? Is the effort required going to drive sufficient output? The effort or 'squeeze' isn't always as hard as we may think. 'Make The Juice Worth The Squeeze!' aims to give simple and effective answers to some of the top people problems that commonly occur for leaders in organisations. Help is often needed to groom leaders to take on higher levels of personal or business performance.

All the topics in this book are about how to build leadership capability. We have chosen to focus on our work with individual leaders rather than teams. However, much of the material contained in the book can also be very useful with teams. For simplicity, tools detailed throughout the book focus on developing individual leadership capability. Our mission is to help people to give their best possible contribution to their business, and stay true to themselves in the process. Managing this development requires several major factors to be in place.

HOW to Use this Book

Leaders in business spend an enormous amount of their time reading and digesting material, to support the decision making and creative process. Information in digestible, bite-size chunks is what they are looking for. Each chapter covers many different aspects of each topic, key points, easy exercises for clarification, pertinent questions to ask, and sample case studies. The bold headlines should make it easy to leaf through the book and locate subjects of particular interest.

Although there are many different ways to tackle an issue, we have chosen to share the type of approach that has been found to be most effective in our experience. Organisations are complex. People are complex. The types of problems that need to be solved are often complex. Therefore, it's quite common for many of these areas to overlap, just as it is common for one person to have needs in several areas.

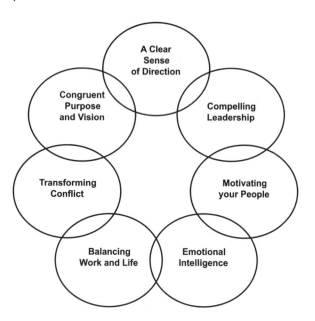

It is not necessary to read the book in sequence, or from cover to cover. Our hope is that this book becomes a reference tool for you. Please feel free to dip into it, in any order, for helpful insights and guidance on specific problems. Because many of the different issues are inter-related though, you might find great value in reading about some of the other aspects that could relate to a particular issue.

Chapter One: Oranges or Lemons?
The Importance of Choosing the Right Personal Direction

First and most obviously, a leader needs to have a firm sense of direction, needs to be clear on their values, their purpose and how that tallies with the organisation. What do you do when you lose the plot? How can you be sure you are in the right place and making the right decisions? What are the pitfalls that get people into trouble, and how can you make better choices? Sometimes making changes can seem daunting. It can feel safer to keep doing what worked in the past, to maintain the status quo. Then there are those difficult dilemmas between a perceived divergence between your purpose and the company's objectives. What is the price of compromise? See chapter one for some insights about how to avoid the trap of success strategies that keep people and organisations at odds.

Chapter two: Top Banana
Increase your Impact and Influence as a Leader

How do great leaders inspire people to want to follow them? What gives them the charisma, gravitas, and confident aura that generates respect? Chapter two reveals how you can develop such influence and impact. Being positive and proactive, having clear values, and credibility are as essential as showing a genuine interest in others, encouraging co-operation and teamwork, and gathering everyone's input in order to make maximum use of talent. Inspiring leaders demonstrate an open and giving attitude. New ideas, innovative thinking and creative solutions are valued. They've mastered the art of communicating simply and asking the right questions. Learn how they think strategically with respect to the political structure, why they value networking, and how they manage their power naturally with quiet authority.

Chapter three: A Plum Job
Motivating your People during Times of Change

Leaders need to be able to motivate and influence their teams, managing both upwards, outwards and downwards. By winning respect, they can generate cohesion amongst their colleagues. Being promoted often means people need to develop more flexible leadership behaviours. How can they improve job satisfaction for both themselves and the team? What 21st Century work practices will help the team give their best? What kind of work environment will lead to improved productivity? It may be a question of moving away from a controlling, dominating, forceful style, towards a more compelling, guiding, inspiring and motivational style. So in order to get the best out of your people, it may be wise to start with yourself. What does your business need now: entrepreneurial drive, leadership or a fresh structure? You'll find a wealth of great input on these subjects in chapter three.

Chapter four: Be the Apple of Everyone's Eye
EQ: the Vital Ingredient for Relationships that Work

Research continues to confirm that one of the most important
factors for success in business is not how intelligent people are
as traditionally measured by a person's IQ (Intelligence
Quotient), but how good they are at managing
themselves and managing the key relationships
in their lives. These areas make up a person's
EQ (Emotional Quotient). Many people are blind
to the areas where they might lack Emotional
Intelligence and are often shocked to discover the
gap between how they see themselves and how
others see them. Equally some highly intelligent, bright,
logical and rational people are bemused when they are unable
to make the impact that they need for success, given their
operational and commercial experience.

There are a few good diagnostic tools on the market. MROI
are certified to use the tool developed by JCA (Occupational
Psychologists) Ltd. Understanding a person's EQ profile makes
it much easier to direct attention, awareness and techniques to
develop and improve that person's Emotional Intelligence. If
you've been curious or confused about what EQ is all about and
how you can improve your own, see chapter four.

Chapter five: The Fruit Salad of Life
How to Juggle your Work / Life Balance

Would you be surprised to know that a major
cause of decreased productivity is overwork?
How many people do you know who long to
live a more balanced life but can't because
of deadlines to meet impossible work targets?
The longer hours people work, the more their
ability to stay focused and productive is impaired,
and the higher their stress. Business pays the price
for this strain on people's performance. High
stress usually leads to increased sick leave. But
it is not only people's health that suffers, it is also
their relationships and families. Although it varies according to
the culture of the company, the trend is now moving towards
more flexibility to meet the changing needs of society. There
are higher expectations that the business can help each
person adapt their role around more flexible hours. If you are
interested in finding ways to think differently about work/life
balance, read chapter five.

Chapter six: The Grapes of Wrath
Does Conflict Enable or Block Progress?

Few people relish conflict in the work place. Few people
enjoy the stress of personality conflicts, hierarchical issues,
negative office politics, frustration with the Board members and
Non-Execs, or behaviours verging on abuse. Most people
would prefer these things didn't happen. When disagreements

occur, what works? When things go wrong, what's the best response? Learn ways to build your reputation with others, by developing your capability to handle unhelpful conflict. You can inspire and influence others and learn how to define what matters. Ultimately, it is how you conduct your arguments more than whether you win or not. Chapter five will give you great tips on how to mature your style as a leader.

Chapter six: Turning Juice into Wine
Create & Communicate the Vision of Your Business

The area that can cause most frustration in business is how a leader can communicate his vision so that everyone in the organisation knows how their efforts contribute to that vision. How can leaders get their message to percolate throughout the company? Clearly, what is needed is to learn how to define a strategic plan that highlights how all departments contribute. Having a clearly defined core purpose, creating a meaningful mission statement to capture the essence of that drive, identifying the strengths, and gathering other perspectives all become crucial elements of this strategy. What can easily be overlooked in the excitement of this process, is whether or not the mission is congruent with the stakeholders. Read chapter six for some excellent guidelines based on tried and tested experience.

The Value of Good Coaching

We know that a book is not a substitute for good internal or external coaching. This book aims to be complementary. Our desire is to increase the value that good coaching can add to an organisation. The development of internal coaching capability is in line with our principle of developing self sufficiency in our client organisations. There should be less need for external coaches in an organisation, if line managers and HR are equipped with the talent and tools to coach effectively.

However, the advantages of employing external consultants should not be overlooked. An external consultant provides a safe, confidential sounding board, someone to challenge your thinking, someone to listen and bounce ideas off. External consultants can add specific depth of expertise without removing the accountability of the decision itself, having another agenda, or over familiarity. Good external consultants can empower the individual and team to be independent and self sufficient beyond the consultancy assignment and into the future.

Talented people are often operating on only a small percentage of their personal power. It is surprising and exciting to liberate this potential! Good coaching can help to accelerate talent and give top people the boost they need. Operating from greater personal power increases the value of these individuals and their contribution in the organisation.

Holding onto top talent, nurturing and grooming them for key roles is one of HR's prime contributions to achieving the organisations goals. Good coaching can support this essential

HR process. Coaching is not therapy. It is not a panacea nor a substitute voice for good line management. Nor is coaching some kind of remedial slap on the hand. Through sharing our combined expertise, knowledge and perspectives, the intention of this book is to support leaders in making their positive contributions. Our aim is to help each person, or team to focus their time, effort, and energy on getting excellent financial, business and personal results, not only for this year, but long term.

The MROI Team

P.S. Our Coaching Needs Analysis on the next two pages will help you get started!

EXERCISE

Shopping List: Needs Analysis for Leadership Development

Focus Area		*Importance to you*				
		Low				*High*

1. Maturing my style as a leader 1   2   3   4   5
2. Balancing my life, given what matters to me now 1   2   3   4   5
3. Establishing and living 'my authentic brand' as
   a leader 1   2   3   4   5
4. Increasing self-awareness and self-management 1   2   3   4   5
5. Improving communication and interpersonal skills 1   2   3   4   5
6. Increasing thinking capabilities and creativity 1   2   3   4   5
7. Managing feedback and understanding how
   I am perceived 1   2   3   4   5
8. Managing my development and career progression 1   2   3   4   5
9. Increasing my power and impact in
   the organisation 1   2   3   4   5
10. Managing stakeholders effectively 1   2   3   4   5
11. Creating a compelling inspirational vision
    and strategy.. 1   2   3   4   5
12. Integrating the mission and vision at all levels 1   2   3   4   5
13. Bullet-proofing the design and execution of a plan 1   2   3   4   5
14. Identifying and articulating the metrics that will
    lift results 1   2   3   4   5
15. Increasing performance of sales and marketing 1   2   3   4   5
16. Reducing non-productive friction and delay within
    the organisation 1   2   3   4   5
17. Improving accountability throughout
    the organisation 1   2   3   4   5

Focus Area	Importance to you				
	Low			*High*	
18. Providing a catalyst for change	1	2	3	4	5
19. Managing and influencing in a matrix structure	1	2	3	4	5
20. Communicating for consistent understanding and action	1	2	3	4	5
21. Encouraging, driving and inspiring innovation at every level	1	2	3	4	5
22. Motivating others	1	2	3	4	5
23. Increasing capability and effectiveness of teams	1	2	3	4	5
24. Increasing speed of joint decision-making	1	2	3	4	5
25. Developing a coaching culture within my team & organisation	1	2	3	4	5
26. Managing diversity	1	2	3	4	5
27. Retaining and developing quality employees long term	1	2	3	4	5
28. Supporting key players to achieve exceptional results	1	2	3	4	5
29. Identifying and accelerating development of new talent	1	2	3	4	5
30. Gathering and acting on employee and management opinion	1	2	3	4	5

If you've circled a lot of high numbers, you may benefit from coaching!

Oranges
or Lemons?

The Importance of Choosing the Right Personal Direction

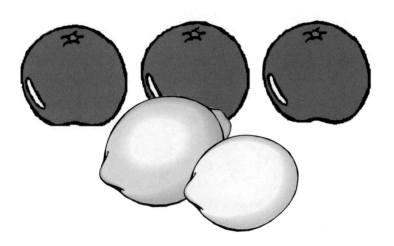

by Arielle Essex

LACK of Personal Direction?

Acquiring a true sense of direction requires knowing your purpose as well as maintaining a flexible attitude towards how to achieve success. The passion and energy that then results generates a power that can overcome all obstacles. Losing your sense of direction can feel devastating, but it could be a great opportunity to re-invent yourself. Stubbornly adhering to old habits and strategies that no longer work just creates diminishing results. Here are some simple, useful questions to help you avoid the traps and effective tools for getting back on track. Getting clarity about your purpose and direction will help you develop more congruence and stability, open up new opportunities, achieve your objectives and raise your leadership capability.

*"Outstanding people have one thing in common:
an absolute sense of mission."*
Zig Ziglar

TOO BUSY to be Successful

Have you ever met someone who has lost their sense of direction? Do you know someone who seems dissatisfied or disappointed? Do they seem to have forgotten why they are doing what they are doing? Do they appear to have lost the plot? Some people seek to impress by being permanently busy all the time. But such busyness often hides the confusion, anxiety or lack of purpose underneath. Maybe you know someone who is just plodding along, stuck in a rut, with no zest for life, low in energy, and lacking enthusiasm? The problem might be: amnesia. They've just forgotten who they are and what they came to do, whether in their work or in their life. Re-discovering your purpose can put the meaning back into life. Your purpose can transform problems into temporary challenges. Clarifying your direction helps you turn every situation into a valuable learning experience. But your true purpose isn't something you do, it is something you live and demonstrate day to day.

People commonly lose their sense of purpose and direction due to a variety of different causes. You may recognise many familiar issues on the following list. How many people can you think of who have complained of being:

- Overworked & overwhelmed
- Stressed & burnt out from too much pressure
- In conflict with colleagues
- Suffering office politics / harassment
- Having no avenue for creativity
- Having no prospect for advancement
- Being in the wrong position
- Stuck in a career choice that's no longer valid
- Struggling with a new phase of life with added challenges
- Feeling the need for change, growth or development
- Feeling demoralised by negative feedback
- Having health Issues / lack of fitness / low energy
- Being out of touch with one's passion, drive & emotions
- Feeling demoralised by a loss of self worth due to events

"Choose a job you love
and you will never have to work a day in your life."
Confucius

Over working and being too busy does not equal success. Productivity declines and good relationships cease to flourish. When too much attention is put on 'Task' and not enough on 'Relationship', the imbalance pulls you off track, nothing prospers despite hard and diligent work. The stress levels increase, conflicts ensue, negative feedback creates bad feelings, career advancement becomes less likely, and it can feel like what was once a dream job is now the wrong position or career altogether. The message is clear: it's time to restore the balance.

The first and most important relationship to foster is the one with yourself. Through re-discovering your purpose, you can put things back into balance and make better decisions according to your highest values. Getting back on track will help you re-connect with your motivation and increase your energy. Knowing what direction to go in, will help you re-invent yourself when it's time to change. As your unique talents, skills and experience evolve, so does your purpose. Ideally, aspire to live your purpose in everything you say and do. Whenever you act in alignment with your purpose, good results, happiness and fulfilment soar.

ULTERIOR Motivations

Being too busy can mask deeper issues so well, that even you don't know what lurks underneath. The effort it takes to just keep up with the workload does not allow you enough time to think. Getting the projects completed, fire fighting, and meeting deadlines can so totally preoccupy your time, that you lose sight of the direction ahead. Whether the pressure comes from achieving success or avoiding failure, the resulting busyness can be blinding.

Here's a little quiz to test yourself about what might be lurking beneath your busyness.

EXERCISE

Have you Fallen into the Trap of Being Too Busy?

1. **What gets dropped out of your diary when you are too busy?**

   Many people neglect to take time for themselves, for exercise, for personal development, for quality time in relationships, for relaxation and having fun or for tuning into their inner vision. Doesn't the cost of being too busy outweigh the benefits of concentrating so much on 'task'? Commit to making the time to get your priorities right, re-define your values and work more efficiently.

2. **How would you be feeling if you weren't so busy?**

   Does being so busy prevent you feeling your true feelings? Do you put off considering difficult decisions or accessing particular avenues of thought? Are you hoping that situations will resolve themselves by not addressing them directly? If you got clear about your personal direction, the answers and solutions appear obvious. Instead of living in denial and avoidance, act from a true place.

3. **What would you be doing if you were not so busy?**

   Are you secretly wishing you were somewhere else, doing something completely different? Although everyone has temporary escape thoughts, like imagining they could fly off on some exotic adventure, does your busyness actually provide a complete distraction to avoid following your true destiny? Are you actually more scared of following your heart's desire than of being bored? If your current role feels like treading water, how long will you continue to do that? How little of your energy and passion may ever find expression? If you knew your true direction, you'd find a way to make it happen. You'd learn how to channel your energy and power more efficiently to produce better results.

4. **How does your busyness provide a convenient excuse?**

Do you get to avoid some other challenge, or not have to face some truth? What if never having the time to develop some skill, talent or ability actually protects you from taking a risk? Is your fear of the next step making you stick your head in the sand of work? Perhaps now is the time for you to re-discover your purpose, step forward and do what fits with your values.

5. **Is being so busy just a disguise for meddling and controlling?**

Do you do too much, and take on too many problems from others because you lack trust? Are you afraid to let go of control, believing no one else will do things as efficiently as you? Learning to trust more, receiving more help from others, and working more interdependently all come much easier when you understand the part you play in the overall plan.

6. **Does your busyness take you in the direction you want and support your purpose?**

   Can you discern the difference between fake busyness and the hard work of true purpose? What signs will let you know you are on or off track? Does your imagination flow? Do inventive ideas and creativity pour out of you? If you stopped being so busy for a moment and opened up to your inner wisdom, you might access some valuable answers.

7. **What would life be like if you weren't so busy?**

   Would you begin to feel less important without the pressure and rushing about? Is there a fear about how others might perceive you in a culture that worships long hours of overworking? Would you lose status or look less ambitious? People in the UK work longer hours than most other countries in Europe. Does being busy mean more efficient or less efficient?

"Whenever you get there,
there's no there there."
Gertrude Stein

FEAR of Success

Many career problems stem from avoiding your purpose. What could be more important than doing what you love most in life? Why would anyone want to resist doing what they are best suited to do? Who would ever want to avoid what brings most fulfilment, happiness and joy in life? Yet so many people create careers and lives full of drudgery, hard work, stress and lack of fulfilment and joy.

Some people think that success is a destination to reach. So they fast track their careers to get there, believing happiness lies somewhere in the future. Going for it feels exciting and exhilarating. But getting there, they fear disappointment! What if they have to change their whole identity, habits, friends and way of being? Suddenly they would be expected to maintain this lofty height of success. What if they reached the pinnacle and then crashed? Better to keep it as an unfulfilled dream than to risk winning and then losing.

Hidden fears about success frequently deter people from following their chosen path. Without realising it, they subtly sabotage their own success. It's more commonly accepted that the fear of failure causes resistance to moving forward. But few people think about what the consequences of success would look like, feel like or what might be expected of them long term. They set off to achieve goals without considering the long term impact or what hidden issues might surface to hold them back from success.

"We generally change ourselves for one of two reasons:
inspiration or desperation."
Jim Rohn

Intelligent people have no problem listing all kinds of goals
that they want to achieve in life. Following classic goal setting
procedures, they know goals need to be phrased in positive,
specific terms. They usually implement ways of measuring
whether or not they are achieving those goals. They also
plan to make good use of their resources, networks, time and
energy to make them happen. But they don't stop to consider
the pre-requisites, presumptions or products that will be the
consequence of those goals. Often these are unspoken and
out of their awareness. How you phrase your goal dramatically
impacts how well you will be able to achieve it.

- **Pre-requisites** refer to the conditions you apply to
  all your decision making and plans. What are you
  willing to do or not do, with regard to the goal you
  have in mind?

- **Presumptions** describe what you presuppose
  will happen. What do you believe will transpire, or
  what do you assume is likely to happen?

- **Products** equal the positive or negative
  consequences that you expect to get as a result of
  achieving this goal. What will happen as a result of
  achieving this goal?

EXAMPLE

Millionaire Mindset

During a coaching session a young business man stated his ambitious goal 'to be a millionaire'. He not only wanted to generate passive income, he also wanted to be happy, healthy and surrounded by beautiful toys, living an exciting live of fun and travel. Although his goal was very positive and clear, more thorough questions revealed some unspoken pre-requisites - the conditions that limited his goal:

He wanted to be a millionaire [pre-requisites]
- as long as he didn't have to work more than 8 hours a day
- as long as he got to do whatever he wanted to do whenever he wanted
- as long as he didn't have to work for someone else
- as long as he liked the nature of the work and it was legal

Oddly enough, his pre-requisites contrasted with several of his presumptions of what was likely to occur. Filling in the unspoken second half of the sentence, he realised that he had some hidden beliefs and considerations working against his desire to achieve this goal.

He wanted to be a millionaire [presumptions]
- (but he didn't believe he could do it)
- (but he'd have to work 18 hour days 7 days a week)
- (but he'd end up doing work he didn't really enjoy)
- (but he wouldn't see his kids grow up)
- (but he'd lose his friends & incur jealousy)

Exploring further, he started thinking about why he wanted to be a millionaire and what end product he really wanted. Could these results be hidden drivers behind his goal?

He wanted to be a millionaire
- so he could live a happy and luxurious life
- so he could be looked up to and admired by all his friends
- so he'd never have to worry about money again
- so he could finally prove he was good enough to his father
- so he could be free
- so he could then fund his favourite ecological projects

Although his goal had seemed so simple, it now appeared to be more complex. These unspoken considerations around his goal could have a profound impact on his progress. After some careful thought, he began to get insights about what he really wanted. He needed a more effective way to think about his goal. So he set about re-phrasing his goal to reflect a more true version of his intent. His new goal: 'I'm creating a flow of abundance that inspires others and contributes to the greater ecology of the whole planet.'

EXERCISE

Clarifying Your Goals

1. List your top goals in a particular context or time frame.

2. For each item on your list, carefully consider the pre-requisites, presumptions and products related to that goal.

> What are you willing to do or not do, related to that goal?

> What are you presuming is likely to happen with regard to that goal?

> What products will be the consequence of achieving that goal?

3. Write these down. If you don't like your answers, feel free to change the way you phrase the goal until you are happy that it reflects your truth.

"Only those who will risk going too far
can possibly find out how far they can go."
T.S. Eliot

OBJECTIVES v Purpose

Company Objectives v an Individual's Purpose

Another problem with direction stems from a divergence
between your perception of the company's objectives and your
purpose. However true this perception might be, clarifying your
direction will help you make the best decisions. Avoid becoming
a source of internal sabotage, or damaging your own reputation.
What if you discovered that you could remain true to your
purpose and find ways that help support positive change rather
than creating conflict?

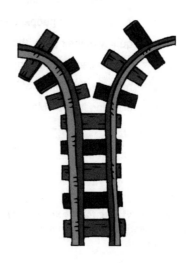

PRICE of Compromise

When practicalities and financial considerations force you to compromise your purpose, it is always at the expense of your fulfilment. Perhaps it is time to re-consider what is more important in your life. Sometimes a temporary sacrifice might be the best solution, but ultimately, what do you want your life to be about? It's so easy to get caught in a rut, particularly about money. Before you know it, ten years have passed. It is important to weigh the costs of investing all your time and energy in pursuits that might fulfil material goals. What does enough look like? It may seem wise to sacrifice now for some future utopia, but what if that tomorrow never comes? Who do you become in the process?

The World Values Survey [www.isr.umich.edu] has studied the relationship between income, success and happiness in 60 countries, representing 75% of the world's population. One conclusion they drew about industrial societies: 'there is practically no relationship between income level and subjective well-being'...especially above the £5,300 income bracket. Although most people believe that more money will improve the quality of their lives, the survey shows that despite increased purchasing power, subjective assessment of 'very happy' levels have declined from 35% to 32%. Are you working harder, but enjoying it less? Maybe it's time for a re-think.

"We are not searching for the meaning of life,
we are searching for the experience of being alive."
Joseph Campbell

CAREER Crossroads

Have you outgrown the parameters of your job specification,
or possibly reached a crossroads in your career? Each new
life phase makes new demands on your time. Having children,
changing relationships, planning retirement or developing
new areas of contribution all require careful re-assessment.
During such transition times, it is good to re-evaluate what is
most important to you. Re-defining your purpose will give you
a clear sense of direction and help you make the right choices.
Exhaustion is sometimes a sign that you have lost sight of what
you truly enjoy. What makes you feel joyful will guide you back
to the state of pure energy. Without joy, you may feel like you
are 'running on empty' no matter how good your intentions may
be. Reviewing your values helps to change your thinking and
connect with a higher vision.

*"We enjoy a thousand material advantages over any generation,
and yet we suffer a depth of insecurity and spiritual doubt they never knew."*
Tony Blair

EXAMPLE

A need to control

One senior manager believed that he 'should' be slick, polished, impressive, and so forceful that success would be inevitable. Unfortunately, he judged his own performance as bumbling, incoherent, amateur and just not good enough, despite receiving great feedback. So this led to him feeling that he 'had to control everything in order to feel safe.' Fearing failure, he struggled to hold on to his polished performance. He described his life as feeling like he was trying to hang onto the side of a rocket that was moving so fast, he might drop off into oblivion if he didn't cling on with every bit of strength he had.

Whenever he felt out of control, he immediately felt helpless and powerless, at the mercy of other people. But this attitude also led him to blame others for everything he could and to use that as an excuse for any lack of success. Sometimes, this then led to the creation of amazing conspiracy theories to explain what was going wrong. These strategies worked very well at keeping him stressed, unsuccessful, powerless and small.

By finding out what he really, really wanted, he was able to get in touch with some of his higher values. He re-discovered his sense of purpose that went beyond being in control. He began to take things less personally, and re-connected with his own inner sense of enduring security. From this more balanced standpoint, he was able to develop a more objective perspective. As his attitude changed, he not only felt less stressed, but found his performance became more relaxed and effective.

What do YOU want?

The Oxford Dictionary defines 'Purpose' as: 'an intended result, something for which effort is being made: an intention to act, determination'. Your purpose is directly linked to all your outcomes and goals. So the quickest way to discover your purpose is to carefully consider your answers to the following questions in the context of your professional contribution and your life as a whole: Take a moment to write down some answers.

> What do you want?
> What do you really want?
> What do you really really want?

You may think that you know what you want, or perhaps it has been so long since you dared to ask such questions, you find it hard to answer. Often life settles into comfortable routines which feel pretty much OK. The only thing you want, is to get rid of a few trouble spots. You want to keep doing what you are doing, but eradicate the problems. Or you may think it pointless to ask these questions. When your life circumstances seem to work against you, you may fall into the trap of believing there are no possibilities for alternative choices. Your zest for life deadens each time you throw away your power to make choices. You cease to be able to tap into your full potential.

Limited thinking comes disguised in different flavours:

1. **Choosing only what seems possible or reasonable**

You justify your decisions with rational sounding arguments, but, in fact, you compromise your purpose. You think too small. Your thinking goes along conventional pathways and doesn't dare to jump out of the box. With so little stretch, there is less enthusiasm and zest.

2. **Choosing the process instead of the result**

You attend trainings to get certificates or letters after your name, rather than actually learning new skills or acquiring knowledge. You tick boxes to look good on paper, but nothing changes in reality. Going through the motions builds pretence, but lacks any true effectiveness.

3. **Choosing conditionally**

You will only choose IF.....Usually you want some guarantee of success or reward. You want to avoid any risk taking. Instead you want assurances, proof, evidence or some other promise of future compensation. This need for security can keep you stuck in outmoded thinking, procedures or positions that no longer fit.

4. **Choosing by Consensus**

You choose what everyone else wants,

compromising your own values in favour of what the team wants or at home, bowing to family considerations. Popular consensus is allowed to drown out the voice of your own inner truth. But the popular vote may or may not be the best solution. Wasn't there an old saying about a camel being a horse created by a committee?

5. Choosing by default

You wait until matters become completely intolerable, circumstances take over, or the decision is made by someone else. Although the passage of time sometimes adds clarity to a situation, more often it means that certain options become unavailable. When there's only one choice left, that's not a choice anymore. If there's no choice, it leads to feeling at the mercy of events, a victim of circumstances, dominated by other forces.

6. Choosing by abdication

You give away your power of choice to some other authority, leaving it to chance or fate. There are times when it's good to let someone else make decisions, but probably not those related to your personal direction. Abdicating your responsibility in making your own choice actually throws away your creative power. Whatever you choose will still be subject to chance and fate. Making a choice means you actually get to participate more in your own life.

If you recognise any of these choices as familiar ways of thinking, let this motivate you to understand yourself better and find the way back to your values. Your enthusiasm, your drive and your stability depend on connecting to your inner truth. This requires a high degree of emotional intelligence, knowing yourself and being in touch with your inner feelings. Ordinary people worry that if they take a risk, they might fail. But what if you take a risk and it all goes well? Making a choice requires an act of faith. Putting your attention on looking good and pleasing others takes a lot less courage than standing up for what you value and believe in. When you fulfil your purpose in everything you do, you will feel more grounded and centred. When you show up, expressing who you really are, you will inspire others to join you in synergy and partnership.

"I believe that the very purpose of our life is to seek happiness. That is clear. Whether one believes in religion or not, whether one believes in this religion or that religion, we all are seeking something better in life. So, I think, the very motion of our life is towards happiness...I believe that happiness can be achieved through training the mind."
Dalai Lama

EXERCISE

Let Your Future Guide You

Have you ever noticed how easy it is to look back in time, and know the right answers with hindsight? If so, this exercise will surprise you. Just imagine you could time travel out to the future and talk to an older, wiser version of you.

By tuning into this more experienced, inner source of wisdom, you can access the part of you that knows what will work, what you should think and say, and what you will be proud that you did. Just choose a quiet space and follow these easy steps:

Current situation

Future situation

1. Assess your current situation, what you want now, whatever considerations you might have, and whatever feelings you are aware of. You can write down a list of all your current goals and objectives if you like.

2. Stand up and leave all those considerations on that chair.

3. Choose another location or chair and pretend you can time travel out into your future.....to a time in the future when you are genuinely living your purpose to the full and enjoying success, happiness and fulfilment. You can visit any age you wish. Often the 99-year-old version of you in the future has some very interesting perspectives.

4. Imagine you could step into the body of this future you, looking out at the world through those eyes, listening, and sensing as if you were this person. Notice how it feels to be in this body, having the beliefs and values of this future you.

5. As you look back towards the you of today, what guidance, advice or insights would you offer? What thinking might need to change? What is your true purpose? What could help you to fulfill that?

6. Be willing to follow or do anything that you feel inspired to do as a result of this advice.

The **SECRET** of Creative Choice

How to be part of the solution rather than being part of the problem

Consciously choosing the results you want requires having a clear vision of your positive outcome. The more your outcomes are aligned with your purpose, the greater your ability to manifest them into reality. The more you can connect with this future self, the more you can feel the energy and guidance supporting you. You can gain as much wisdom from tapping into the future, as you can from accumulating experience from the past. Consciously choosing is the active form of commitment. It is an ongoing process rather than a one time event. Every moment presents you with new opportunities to choose. If you make a mistake, just choose again and correct it. When you commit, you can focus and direct your energy in a true direction. Without commitment, your energy and goals get split into many directions, dissipating your energy and weakening your strength. Consciously choosing supports partnership, trust and success.

EXERCISE

Discover your purpose

1. Choose 3 outcomes that you feel passionate about, large or small – anything you want. Write each one at the top of a page, making sure it is succinct. You can draw a box around it if you like. Then for each one carefully consider your answers to the following questions.

2. Imagine for a moment that you have already achieved this outcome. Then ask yourself:
What does having this do for me? What does it give me?
Draw an arrow downwards from your Outcome box and write your answer below.

3. Considering what you just wrote down and imagine you have already achieved that, fully and completely. Then ask yourself:
What does achieving that allow me to do?
Draw an arrow downwards the previous answer and write your new answer below.

4. Then imagine you are already doing that in just the way you always wanted to, and ask yourself:
What does doing this allow me to achieve?
Draw an arrow downwards from your last answer and write your new answer below.

5. Thinking about having achieved this outcome fully and completely, ask yourself:

What does this allow me to do or experience?

Draw an arrow downwards from your last answer and write your new answer below.

6. Visualising yourself having done this outcome fully and completely, ask yourself:

What does this allow me to be?

Your answers should look something like this:

OUTCOME: What do you want?

If you got this what would it do for you?

If you got [Answer 2] what would this give you?

If you got [Answer 3] what does this allow you to experience?

If you got [Answer 4] what does this allow you to achieve?

If you got [Answer 5] what would this allow you to do?

If you got [Answer 6] what would this allow you to be?

7. After repeating these questions for each of your 3 original outcomes, look for some similarities in your answers. Circle any outcomes have the same meaning. Every outcome you write down reveals what you consider most important: your values. If you'd like, you can put these words together into a sentence to create a statement of Purpose. Or alternatively, choose something to symbolise the meaning for you metaphorically: an object, geometric shape, plant, animal, etc.

8. Safety check: what would happen if you lived your Purpose fully? What else would have to change in your life? Would this be OK? How would this affect others? What would change in your community, workplace, country or planet if you lived your Purpose? Think about how you could deliver your Purpose through what you are already doing. You might realise you have already been doing just that. How could you do it even better?

When you realise all the ways you have already been living your purpose, you may begin to find it easier to trust your intuition more. Instead of forcing outcomes, you can be flexible knowing you are going in the right direction. You can let go more and enjoy the feeling of fulfilment in everything you do, whether it is astonishingly successful or not. By being more aware of your purpose, you can find new ways to express it, or give it - in every little thing you do. Your purpose can make you unstoppable. It will give your life more meaning. But perhaps best of all, becoming more aligned with your purpose will give you courage, vitality and energy for everything you are.

DEALING with the Have-Tos

Whenever you've been resisting your purpose, denying yourself the opportunities to follow your heart, chances are your inner gremlin has given you a hard time. If you have a voice inside your head that keeps telling you that you 'have to', 'should', 'ought to', 'must' do what you don't want to do, this sets up an inner conflict. Such an inner battle wastes your energy. Confronting such an inner gremlin only intensifies the battle. It is far more effective to simply thank it for sharing and continue to move towards your purpose. Give yourself permission to feel whatever you are feeling, let your gremlin say whatever it wants to say, and overlook old repetitious remarks. You could also ask what it needs in order to allow you to continue to focus on your purpose. Don't suppress or ignore it. Just keep your focus on moving towards your purpose, and this inner resistance will lose its power.

"Leaders must learn to discipline their disappointments.
It is not what happens to us, it is what we choose to do about what happens
that makes the difference in how our lives turn out."
Jim Rohn

LIFE Goals

A classic graph with a new twist

Your Direction may include many different types of goals in the various aspects of life. When you score high in several categories, life is good! When you consider all the different realms of your life, how high would you score yourself in the following categories? After you have assessed each area, note down what changes you have made and what inspired you. Create your own graph so you can see at a glance which areas might need more attention.

Achievement goals:
What accomplishments you're proud of
Relationship goals:
How full of love & friendship & happy you are
Material goals:
What you have acquired - home, money, toys etc
Physical goals:
How well you've looked after your fitness and health
Challenge goals:
How you grow, learn, develop personally
Enjoyment goals:
How much fun, exploration, travel, adventure
Contribution goals:
What you give to make the world a better place
Spiritual goals:
How you see yourself as part of a greater picture

EXERCISE

Steps to drawing some valuable insights

1. Draw a circle and divide it into as many segments as you think you may need – it's better to have a few left over rather than not enough.

2. Decide which areas of your life you want to plot on the graph and write words to describe each one, in each segment.

3. Consider each area separately and intuitively assess how well you think you are doing on a scale of 0 – 10.

4. Mark a line across the segment to indicate how well you are doing. You can colour the full part of the segment in, if you like.

5. Repeat the process with each of the segments and then you can see at a glance which areas of your life are doing well, and which may require more attention.

6. Now think of each of those areas: What are the most valuable changes you have made in the last year or so in that area?

7. What inspired those changes and what helped you to make them?

8. What changes would you like to make in each area?

9. How do these add more insight to your purpose and direction?

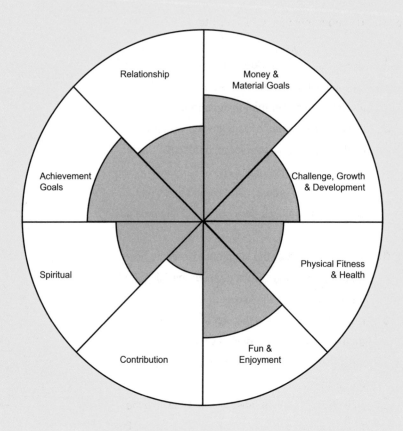

"Great things are not done by impulses,
but by a series of small things brought together."
Van Gogh

STUCK in a Rut

Would you be surprised to know that the most difficult strategies to change are successful strategies? You can probably name a few companies that once achieved great success by having a very clear sense of direction but later failed. Believing they knew the right formula, they followed the same success strategy for years. It always worked in the past, so they assumed it must be the right way to do things, so they doggedly continued. When the going got tough, they just did more of what worked before, not stopping to notice that things had changed. They didn't take stock of new developments, different requirements, or evolving needs. Instead, they put even more energy and drive into the same old strategies. Then they were surprised when their previous success turned into failure.

Perhaps you've noticed how hard it can be to shift your own habits and what used to be successful strategies. What once worked well may no longer get you the results you want. Or what excited you ten years ago, no longer feels satisfying now. Similarly, being promoted to a new position often requires a whole new level of leadership skills. People who fail to grasp that they need to change their habits often make the classic mistake of repeating their old behaviours long past their effectiveness. Isn't the definition of madness doing the same thing again and again, expecting a different result?

"It is not the strongest of the species that survive, nor the most intelligent, but the one most responsive to change."
Charles Darwin

FAILING to Respond

'It's like stepping on the gas while the wheel of the car is stuck and spinning in the mud' says Professor Donald Sull of Harvard Business School. In his book 'Revival of the Fittest', Dr. Sull talks about why companies go bad and how great managers can remake them. His systematic research into how companies respond to change has revealed that many companies fail because they rely too much on the original formulas that brought their initial success. They may see the changes coming, but fail to respond effectively. Some never respond at all. Being responsive to your own inner changes means regularly taking stock, getting feedback, reviewing your values, being objective and willing to be flexible.

EXAMPLE

Internal conflict

A highly successful scientist who used to enjoy his work, no longer found his career challenging. He thought there must be more to life than work and spending money. What puzzled him was that he was used to being a person of strong ambitions with great ability to make things happen. He counted himself as one of the lucky people who had actually achieved his childhood dream: designing space missions for Nassau. He had enjoyed every part of his journey of achievement. But after many years relishing his successful career at Nassau, he felt he had 'done that'. It was time for change. He didn't want to continue down the same route for the next 20 years.

Because of his keen ambition to work on space missions, his whole life had seemed like a road with very high hedges on either side. It felt like he had never seen the sky, nor the fields, nor the other paths he could have taken. Now, when he dreamed of being more spontaneous and making changes, he felt scared, out of control, overwhelmed and unable to cope. Inside his head, a continuous battle raged between two voices: one urging him to just 'get away!' and the other reminding him he had to pay his mortgage. His adventurous-loving, freedom voice wanted to escape, do something new and exciting. But his practical family-loving side needed to honour his responsibilities.

After some exploration, it became clear that 'getting a life' was his highest priority. He carefully explored and re-defined his purpose until he began to trust his ability to feel what was right for him again. Gradually, he gained more certainty in creating his new direction. Much to his surprise, he realised that he didn't need to make external drastic changes as much as he needed to change his internal attitude. To 'get a life' now meant enjoying everything he had, feeling grateful and connected to something bigger than himself. He relaxed and began to enjoy exploring different avenues, content in the knowledge that he could satisfy off of his requirements without upsetting the balance of his whole family.

"Nothing stops an organisation faster
than people who believe that the way you worked yesterday
is the best way to work tomorrow."
Jon Madonna

SUCCESSFUL Formulas for Failure

People tend to make the same mistake in their jobs that they make in their personal lives, so it is not surprising that companies reflect this too. Getting stuck happens slowly, long before you realise something's not quite right. Familiar routines become addictive because the security of knowing what's what feels good. The problem starts when you become committed to:

- a particular role – your identity is stuck in a box
- a strategy that works – you do the same thing again and again
- a methodology – you trust it will work even though it doesn't
- a special technology – you think the new gizmo will solve it
- a resource or supplier – you depend on their service alone
- a key customer or product – becomes 90% of your business

These commitments constitute a success formula. Because it worked before, you stubbornly believe it will work again. It's like being married to the past. It doesn't make sense to divorce yourself from the formula that once worked. The commitments that used to be positive now become a trap. When there are too many commitments, the situation appears complex, but in fact, you have four choices:

1. **Keep doing what you are doing**. It worked before, so if you keep plugging away, sooner or later, it might work again. Anyway, it is familiar, comfortable and everything is set in place to keep going. You may rationalise that it could cost too much to change it anyway. Unfortunately times have changed, and what used to work so well probably won't be sufficient to meet new demands and needs. You need to break out of this comfort zone.

2. **Spin off into other ventures** to attack the problem and satisfy the need. Rather like having an affair to solve a marriage problem, this is usually expensive and rarely helps the situation. Plus you'll probably run into the same problems again with the new venture because you haven't changed the strategies that were causing the original problem.

3. **Throw out all the old commitments** and start all over again from scratch – often a very expensive solution in time, effort and money. The high risk element may feel exciting at first. You may be able to pull it off. A completely new venture may require you to change all your old ways, but if you don't, the old problems will resurface in a new guise.

4. **Change the success formula** by responding to what the current situation demands. Stop following

the status quo, re-assess the direction that aligns with your purpose and re-commit. When the pain of **not** changing is higher than the cost of changing, the old economic drivers can be overcome. Heightened awareness plus responsiveness to current needs that's in alignment with values - that works.

"You can never change things
by fighting the existing reality.
To change something, build a new model
that makes the existing model obsolete."
R.B. Fuller

The RIGHT Commitment?

How can you determine which commitments are right for a specific situation? Can you ever be sure? Can success ever be guaranteed? How can you ensure that the new commitments stick and there is no backsliding into old status quo behaviour? Certainly, there are risks in making changes, but there are may be bigger risks in not changing. What often helps is to take a more global perspective. View the situation the way the rest of the world will see it. Instead of looking through your old spectacles, imagine you could look through an objective video camera. How does each decision fit into the bigger, more global picture?

"The way to succeed
is to double your failure rate."
Thomas Watson, IBM chief

FAILURE as a Learning Tool

High achievers are often perfectionists who take great pride in their flawless performance. A useful acronym I heard recently was that F.A.I.L. stands for 'First Action In Learning'. Inevitably, mistakes will happen along the path to achieving success. How you choose to respond, what you learn and how flexible you can be will determine the final outcome. When you stay connected to your inner purpose and direction, you will be more resilient and able to handle whatever comes your way. Feelings of distress, self attack, defeat, depression, and low self worth may tempt you to give up. Just remember you can treat any failure as an opportunity to learn and benefit, and you'll sail through difficult times. Assume that whatever happens has some positive benefit, sooner or later.

EXERCISE

Your Worst Failures or Your Best Learning Opportunities?
If you are not convinced that you've learned from previous mistakes, or some event still seems to be the worst thing that could have happened, it could be that the learning process is not yet complete. Reflect on these questions:

1. Recall some specific past failures in your work, your relationships or your life. Start with a small one first for practice.

2. What lessons did you learn from this event? How well did you learn the lessons - or did they need to be repeated?

3. How have you changed or evolved as a result of this? What do you value differently now? What may still need further work?

4. In what ways have you matured, enlarged your understanding or deepened your wisdom? Have you become stronger in some way?

5. How has this helped you to make better decisions for the future? In what ways are you already behaving differently?

6. Have you fully considered the positive intentions of each person involved? What did each person believe they were achieving or defending for themselves?

7. Have you explored other perspectives? Think of someone you truly admire and respect. How would they handle this situation?

8. How did your expectations, thoughts, behaviour or communication contribute to this situation occurring? What could be a better choice?

Some lessons come with expensive price tags. The bigger the pain, the more profound the learning. The longer you stay in a place of blame, or self recrimination, the longer you suffer and the slower you progress. Reviewing difficult events to extract all the learning you can, will save you repeating the same mistakes again.

> *"Here is a test to find out whether your mission in life is complete.*
> *If you're alive, it isn't."*
> Richard Bach

COPING During Unpredictable Times

The addiction to the fast pace of progress means that demands and pressure will continue to increase. The relentless expectations of where people think they should be, how their career should have progressed, what they should have achieved by each milestone makes them live by the clock. As they chase the next goal, constantly fearing that they are not progressing fast enough, the stress levels soar. Crowded schedules drive people faster and faster until no one can keep up. But as psychologist Robert Holden says, 'Doing things fast isn't always the quickest way to success'.

Clarity about your direction must come first. Then your purpose will help determine which requirements need to be considered. Your values will govern what your new commitments should be. And consequently, your priorities should flow naturally from all of these decisions. Commitments aligned with your direction, values and purpose will always support and sustain you, helping you stay sane and calm in turbulent times. Stay vigilant and beware of the warning signals that let you know when the balance gets off kilter:

Avoid:

1. Having too many commitments
2. Doing what worked last time or in the last job
3. Relying on something because it works in theory
4. Copying what seemed to work for someone else
5. Failing to run the numbers
6. Not sweating the details
7. Failing to act fully on recognised problems

8. Ignoring core values
9. Delegating the hard work
10. Sticking with new commitments past their sell-by date

Aim to be less busy and more effective, to do less and achieve more. Schedule in regular time to reflect and tune into your purpose and direction as a priority. How can you work smarter instead of longer and harder? Get rid of time wasters, reduce the pressure and free up your time and energy to be more creative and inspired. Keep things as simple as possible.

It takes great courage to maintain your direction. It requires a steady, balanced, flexible and consistent follow-through to see changes through to completion. Along the way there could be many risks, the situation may become unstable, there could be distractions and temptations, the finances could be jeopardised. But by staying aligned with your purpose and following your inner direction, you will inspire trust and credibility. Remember the time honoured idea that 'success is a state of mind'. Your thoughts and intentions, based on your inner truth, transmit great energy, giving birth to good feelings and leading to positive actions. By having a clear sense of direction, you will be able to make the best choices. Success will inevitably follow.

> *"If mankind is not to perish after all the dreadful things it has done and gone through, then a new spirit must emerge. And this new spirit is coming not with a roar but with a quiet birth, not with grand measures and words but with an imperceptible change in the atmosphere - a change in which each one of us is participating."*
> Albert Schweitzer

Top Banana

Increase Your
Impact & Influence
as a Leader

by Arielle Essex

GREAT Leaders

Great leaders inspire respect, support and cooperation. Their words have impact. They influence others with ease and set examples for everyone to follow. When a leader exudes that positive, 'going-for-it' energy, obstacles melt away. Such leadership skills can be learned. By clarifying your focus, adopting the right attitude, using the most effective delivery, communicating clearly and thinking strategically, your leadership ability will soar. Here are some useful tips to empower you as a leader.

INFLUENCE and IMPACT

Good leaders know how to create impact by radiating charismatic authority. They influence others indirectly without confrontation or alienation. As they forge new pathways, people willingly follow, trusting their judgement. Good leaders inspire respect, loyalty, support and enthusiasm. Because they also have the good humour to engage with others and listen well, they are liked. They can also be very direct and forthright. But their sensitivity helps them pace others, pick up crucial information, bring people along with them, and get the timing right.

People are not born with influencing skill, they learn it.

Unfortunately, some leaders lack these skills. Their great ideas get shot down by sceptics, only to be adopted later on by someone else who gets all the credit. Their arguments get dismissed without proper consideration. Their timing is off. They never feel heard or taken seriously. They struggle to get co-operation and agreement. Despite hard work, intelligence, competence and preparation, they lack credibility.

"You can buy a person's hands but you can't buy his heart.
His heart is where his enthusiasm, his loyalty is."
Stephen Covey

What do you have to do to be taken seriously? Did you know that different people require different styles of communication? How easy is it for you to turn objections, resistance, doubts or denial into agreement? What if there was a secret way to convince sceptics? Wouldn't it be great to know how to phrase your message to reach people, and then direct them to where they need to be?

Some of the following ideas, strategies and suggestions may already be familiar to you. But some of the new research and practical techniques may surprise you with their immediate effectiveness. The only way to know if these will work for you or not is to test them out for yourself.

"The task of the leader is to get his people from where they are to where they have not been."
Henry Kissinger

NFLUENCE: The 3 Essential Elements

Perhaps you've noticed that lasting influence has nothing to do with a job title or position in the company. Influence also has nothing to do with being manipulative, aggressive, ambitious or opportunistic. Although high positions in a company naturally wield power, a person with the right approach can influence from any position.

Having this kind of influence requires:

1. **Authentic Leadership**
Be consistent, direct & rigorous

2. **Language of Influence**
Be both flexible and effective

3. **Positive Politics**
Alliance with the right network

ONE: Authentic Leadership

Natural influence radiates from authenticity. People want to follow leaders of integrity, clarity and power. Leaders they can admire and trust. Leaders who embody their values, understand the immediate issues and have a farsighted and positive vision of the future. There is nothing more compelling than someone totally committed to achieving an outcome. Ending slavery, putting a man on the moon, and countries winning their independence, all required charismatic leaders who could convince people that the time was right for change.

"A leader is a dealer in hope. "
Napoleon Bonaparte

Influence with INTEGRITY

A leader who wants to have more influence must start with the
right mind set. You may have come across presenters who had
great style as orators, but their message lacked substance,
their arguments were weak or their integrity was questionable.
So before considering making improvements to your style
of delivery, you might want to check that you have resolved
any inner conflicts you might have. Are your values, direction,
purpose and vision grounded in reality?

Components of the Inner Mind Set

- Clear Purpose, Vision & Direction
- Congruent Values: within oneself & with the
  company
- Sees both the Big Picture & the Details
- Passionate, enthusiastic and positive
- 100% committed and co-operative
- Sees things through to completion
- Sets an example of integrity, honesty & justice
- Inspires, motivates and empowers others
- Likeable, good humoured, easy to engage with
- Intuitive, decisive and wise

"Lead and inspire people.
Don't try to manage and manipulate people.
Inventories can be managed but people must be lead."
Ross Perot

EXAMPLE

The Devil in the Detail

The Vice President of a large bank, with an impressive track record and great management style, had one problem area. She kept getting negative feedback on her presentations. Her grasp of detail, her memory and strategic thinking were phenomenal. She had the best intentions to communicate in depth, as she reported the detailed accounts during the regular international meetings. Talking almost faster than she could think, she rarely made any mistakes. But to her dismay, she lost most of her audience as she sprinted through page after page of information.

Reviewing what occurred, I asked her 'Who in the audience actually needed to have the detail of what she was presenting?' It turned out that only 3 or 4 out of the 50 people in the room needed to know the details. The rest would have been much happier just receiving a 'big picture' version with a focus on the bottom line. As she thought this over, she realised she had been driven by her belief that she needed to cover all the bases and prove how she had reached her conclusions.

For her next presentation, she decided to prepare a written report covering all the details to hand out to those who needed them, and then constructed a much more dynamic presentation summarising what was going on with the conclusions she had drawn. With much less detail to squeeze into her time slot, she would able to speak at a normal pace and keep her audience with her.

CONGRUENT Values

When you want to be taken seriously, carefully consider what is most important for you. Your values are what make you uniquely you. There's no use pretending you are something different. When the pressure is on and the orange gets squeezed, out comes....orange juice! Not apple juice or wine. No matter how well you think you can hide your feelings, or pretend you believe otherwise, your inner state seeps out and will be transmitted to others. So, check out your underpinning values with your Coach or just take some time to reflect on the following questions.

Quick Check: Are your Values congruent?

1. What qualities are important to me? What values do I stand for?

2. Are these values relevant now, or do they need to be updated?

3. Do my actions, words & behaviours support those values?

4. Are there any gaps between those values & the choices I make?

5. Am I kidding myself, or repressing or distorting any information?

6. Are my values aligned with the company's values?

7. Am I 100% committed to my values? If not, what needs to be different?

KNOW what you want

You probably already know everything you need to know about goal setting. What's even more important than clarity though, is maintaining your focus when the going gets tough. Perhaps you've seen projects start out with great purpose only to get distracted off course and lose their way. What kind of focus does it take to stay on track no matter how much zig zagging might occur? How can a leader keep it simple? Susan Scott, author of 'Fierce Conversations' suggests some simple questions to guide your thinking and help maintain your direction even in the most complex situations.

Questions to maintain the focus

Where are we going?

Why are we going there?

Who is going with us?

How are we going to get there?

Are we maximising potential?

Are we using all our capabilities?

Are there resource implications?

Who needs to know and know what?

"Do not follow where the path may lead.
Go instead where there is no path and leave a trail."
Ralph Waldo Emerson

EXERCISE

Thought Leadership

Mastering skills, following well established procedures and developing competence will take you only so far. What marks a leader is fresh, innovative, broad minded thinking. Instead of repeating the same old tried and trusted ways, leaders of today need to have their fingers on the pulse, sensitive to fast changing markets and ready to think creatively, be open to new ideas and take risks. How well would you score yourself on the following?

Score Yourself 1 - 10

Discerning, wise, grounded & intelligent 1 2 3 4 5 6 7 8 9 10

Original, creative, lateral thinking 1 2 3 4 5 6 7 8 9 10

Innovative, open to new ideas 1 2 3 4 5 6 7 8 9 10

Paints a compelling & practical future 1 2 3 4 5 6 7 8 9 10

Listens & gathers information thoroughly 1 2 3 4 5 6 7 8 9 10

Sensitively paces others
   & brings them along 1 2 3 4 5 6 7 8 9 10

Welcomes appropriate change
   & takes calculated risks 1 2 3 4 5 6 7 8 9 10

Communicates decisions clearly 1 2 3 4 5 6 7 8 9 10

"The space between thoughts is the place
where insight can make itself known."
Deepak Chopra

The SECRET Ingredient

The Secret Ingredient: A Compelling Delivery

Surprisingly, over ninety percent of communication and impact depends on style of delivery. You're probably well aware that a person's beliefs, values, and expectations, are all revealed sub-consciously through facial expression, voice tone, movement and energy. This why it is so crucial to start with clear purpose, direction and intention. Inner conflicts destroy congruence. Whenever there's lack of conviction or a focus on the negative, you lose power and engender fear, doubt and confusion.

Top Tip:

Before you begin any communication, it's a good idea to be crystal clear on your conversational objective: what do you want from this conversation? Then adopt the right state and approach to achieve that.

Ineffective delivery style not only detracts from the message, but may be perceived as ignorance. Perhaps you've had the experience of sitting through presentations feeling bored or distracted by strange mannerisms and verbosity. Despite a person having high levels of competence, knowledge and preparation, poor communication habits may risk losing the audience, not being heard, and not being taken seriously.

Conversely, a compelling delivery can give importance and value to the simplest message. People sit up and take notice. The speaker appears confident, competent, highly intelligent and gets the whole room to agree with ease. What could you gain by learning some simple tips to make your message irresistible?

EXAMPLE

Negative Feedback

When a senior manager was promoted to work in a new district, he was surprised and dismayed to receive negative feedback about his aggressive and bullying style. This had never happened in the past, so he was mystified. As he walked into the room for our first meeting, part of the problem seemed obvious. Because his hobby was weight lifting, he had muscles bulging out of his shirt with a short neck, upright posture and movements that were somewhat stiff. His head was shaved, and he maintained a very serious facial expression. It was easy to imagine that some people might have felt intimidated just looking at him.

Unfortunately, in his desire to do a good job in the new position, he had been taking extra care to seriously focus on the tasks at hand, without paying enough attention to building good relationships. His people simply had not had a chance to get to know him and find out what a nice person he really was.

We filmed him doing role plays and during meetings so that he could see what he looked like. He was astonished and understood the problem immediately. In fact, he had a great smile, good sense of humour and genuine caring and liking for his people. All he needed was to let them know that. So he practiced making his delivery style more approachable and friendly. He had no further problem with negative feedback.

Revealing BEHAVIOURS

The Behaviours that Reveal Inner State

- How you stand or sit
- How you move and walk
- The openness of your body
- How you look at people
- Your gestures and nods
- Your facial expressions
- Where you focus
- Speed of talking
- Your voice tone
- Your breathing

"The price of greatness is responsibility."
Winston Churchill

Congruence: How to be HEARD

Most people don't pay much attention to what they do with their posture, gestures, facial expressions and how they speak. The mistake they make is thinking that changing their usual habits would make them less real or authentic. This is as mis-guided as believing that if you say something and the other person doesn't understand you, it's their fault. If you have an important message to get across, it deserves to be delivered in a way that is congruent to that meaning. The way you choose to say it also depends on who you are talking to. Perhaps you've had the experience of watching someone switch off in the middle of your important communication. Different people have different styles of listening and thinking. If you use the wrong delivery style, you might as well be speaking a foreign language.

Top Tip:
If someone doesn't understand your message the way you meant it, it's your job to change the communication until they get what you mean.

CATS or DOGS?

People are complex. Luckily, there is an easy way to unravel the differences. According to Michael Grinder, author of *'Charisma, The Art of Relationship'*, you can simplify matters by dividing all human behaviour into two metaphorical types: CATS or DOGS. Using these well known household pets helps clarify complicated internal processing and choice of behaviour. If the person you are talking to demonstrates more CAT or DOG behaviour, it's best to modify your approach accordingly. This not only improves rapport, but greatly increases understanding and cooperation. The aim is to be perceived as both credible and approachable.

When you consider the stereotyped qualities of ordinary cats and dogs, you'll discover you already know a great deal about the behaviours that hold the secret to creating charisma, influence, and impact. CATS tend to be aloof, haughty, quiet, still, in control, focused on their own interests, and quite happy to be alone. DOGS are gregarious, friendly, barking or panting a lot, constantly active, and happy to please and follow a master.

You can't teach a CAT, punish him or reward him - he just ignores you and carries on doing whatever he wants. A DOG can be taught lots of tricks and he typically overreacts to both punishment and rewards. Fights between the two are usually won by CATS.

DOGS both fear and provoke CATS.

In the general population, 70% of people demonstrate DOG types of behaviour most of the time. The CATS, although a minority, quickly rise to the top in terms of power and control. CATS like being leaders and DOGS are happier following, as long as the CAT is doing a good job. Any competent individual can lead DOGS because they are innately co-operative. Influential leaders need to develop the skills to be able to manage CATS of all levels. The trick is to attract CATS to participate and get them to want to join you.

Top Tip:
Remember people change their behaviour according to context, objective and who they are with. Choose your response to meet their energy appropriately in the moment.

The TWO Styles of Behaviour

[With acknowledgement to Michael Grinder]

	Credible CAT	Approachable DOG
Confidence v. Competence:	more confident than than competency warrants	more competent than confident
Attitude to Power:	comfortable with it	shies from it
Attitude to Conflict:	rises to it	confused / avoids it
Seeks:	promotion / challenge	comfort
Traits:	ambitious	vulnerable
Likes:	change, risk, new options, difference	tried & trusted ways safety, security
Goal:	the outcome and productivity of group	good relationships: people are important
People:	are held accountable	are highly accepted
Decision style:	decides internally for self	asks others opinion
Management style:	intervenes early	intervenes much later
Decisions:	loves to decide	prefers info gathering
Creativity:	desires new ideas	likes problem solving

Every person has both CAT & DOG capability. Both are useful in different situations. So, although people do show consistent preferences in certain contexts, it is important to remember not to typecast a person as behaving like only a CAT or only a DOG. Just focus on what behaviour is being demonstrated in the moment. Also, there are varying degrees of CAT & DOG.

One the next page is a graph to depict the difference between the two extremes of CAT & DOG. This indicates an analogue scale with various degrees of CAT & DOG qualities as you move up and down the diagonal line. Just like there are different types of Cats and Dogs, there are different degrees of Cat and Dog behaviour in people. An overly friendly Labrador may be at the bottom left extreme end of the scale, moving up to a German Shepherd or Poodle towards the centre of the graph. Then the friendliest, soppy Tabby Cat might be at the bottom end of the Cat line moving up to a cool Siamese at the top right.

The Dog end of the scale represents how Approachable a person is in their behaviour. The Cat end of the scale represents the degree of Credible behaviours displayed. Remember there are many more Dogs than Cats. Dogs become followers and Cats become leaders in an organization.

Cat v Dog GRAPH

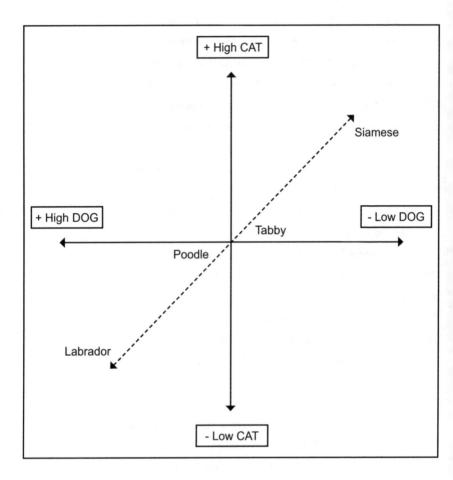

PERMISSION

The ideal for increasing charisma, rapport and influence is
to be able to demonstrate either CAT or DOG behaviour as
necessary. You then become a valuable 'liaison' who both
CATS & DOGS will listen to and willingly follow. Knowing which
style to use depends on how much 'permission' you have
from moment to moment. When people feel comfortable and
open, there is more permission to communicate openly. Less
permission requires being more formal and careful. Depending
on what signals the other person sends, you need to respond
accordingly.

Take Care of DOGS

The people in your organization who demonstrate lots of DOG behaviour are the lifeblood of the company. They are the loyal 'people people' who thrive on relationship. They love doing a good job, value competence & expertise, and can be trusted to follow well established procedures. They are good team players who like to gather information and listen to everyone's opinions before coming to a decision. They do well at handling complex detail and love problem solving. But despite high levels of competence, education, degrees and expertise, they often lack confidence. They don't feel qualified enough to wield power, although they secretly expect to be promoted on the merit of their contribution. DOGS are so co-operative and easy to get along with, a leader can count on their support and expect little difficulty.

"Outside of a dog, a man's best friend is a book;
inside of a dog, it is very dark."
Groucho Marx

How DOGS try to Win Arguments

Just like a guard dog barking at an intruder, a passionate DOG wins arguments by using an intense debating style. Armed with detailed ammunition, a highly competent DOG will fire off point after point, talking faster than a machine gun. They believe if they keep talking, no one will be able to interrupt them. Their facts and evidence are impressive, usually irrefutable and exhausting. Think about a heated debate in the House of Parliament. Listeners under this kind of siege will find it hard to breathe, let alone slip a word in. Some motivational speakers use this style to fire up their audience and demolish opposition. It works, but often generates stress in both the speaker and the listener. Learning some CAT techniques for charismatic influence might be more effective in some situations.

Influencing DOGS

Because DOGS value relationships, they want everyone to get along and be happy. You can enhance your relationship with them by making the time to chat and be friendly. Because they need to feel liked, they do not respond well to harsh feedback or criticism. Be agreeable, show personal interest, remember birthdays, appreciate and compliment their good work as much as possible. A friendly work environment and a good training programme that satisfies their love of learning may be more motivating than a reward scheme.

Because DOGS want everyone to be happy, they often fall into the trap of making allowances for others' mistakes. They will accommodate, accommodate, accommodate bad behaviour beyond the norm, silently repressing their anger and sense of injustice. Perhaps you've experienced someone whose anger suddenly crossed the threshold where they could no longer contain it. When DOGS explode in genuine rage, it is difficult to make amends. This is best avoided by treating them with the care and sensitivity to make sure their needs get met.

EXAMPLE

Consequences of Mis-Reading a Dog:

A senior executive felt her role had become so specialized
that she had become side lined. Despite years of loyal service,
she now watched newcomers leapfrog into positions of power
above her, while her own future development stood still.
Highly competent, with massive expertise, she stood out in the
company as one of a kind. Secretly, she wished that her good
track record would be rewarded by having some extraordinary
position bestowed upon her.

The Board valued her immensely, but remained blind to her
predicament. They enjoyed the revenue she brought in though,
and didn't want to lose her. When the HR Director discovered
her discontent, a 360 was arranged to help assess her talent
and possibilities for advancement. Although most of the
feedback from the 360 was incredibly positive, a few comments
echoed her worst fears. It seemed that others had noticed that
her position had become a dead end. She suspected comments
were being made behind her back.

Unfortunately, instead of taking a proactive stance or initiating
the crucial conversations with key people to rectify the matter,
she ruminated, allowing her anger to grow until it went
over threshold. Massively over reacting to events, she then
threatened to leave the company. The Board was surprised
and horrified, since there had been no obvious preamble to
this situation. If only they had recognised the signs at an earlier
stage, they would not have had to work so hard to pacify her
anger or risk losing this top talent.

Key Points When Approaching DOG:

Approachable traits such as rapport and trust are often by-products of a person feeling known and appreciated. Leaders need to be genuine, real and authentic. They show they care by:

- Showing interest in personal relationships and asking about latest developments in their world.

- Good listening skills: being fully present when listening and maintaining eye contact, saying encouraging words 'uh huh', 'yes' etc.

- Remembering people's birthdays and special occasions.

- Acknowledging people's contributions with emotive appreciation.

- Avoid issuing commands. When possible, ask them to do a 'favour' for you.

- Avoid reprimands, criticism or punishment whenever possible.

- Be less formal in speech, dress and behaviours, nodding, smiling, gesturing.

Talking 'DOG' Body Language

Be more personable, and use natural eye contact when talking to DOGS. Lean forward, nod your head and say 'uh, huh' to encourage the speaker and let him know you are listening. This comes across as more approachable and friendly. Be more casual, less formal and stiff in your posture, dress and manners. Be less distant and more relaxed. Stand and sit asymmetrically, tilt your head. Smile, share jokes and laughter, be sociable.

Instead of giving orders, ask them to do a 'favour' for you, and get them to feel they are helping you out. They like feeling they are doing something out of loyalty and friendship. Never be curt, avoid asking them a lot of questions or putting them on the spot. Instead, give them choices. Ask them questions with multiple choice answer possibilities. Also avoid reprimands and punishment whenever possible as DOGS are easily hurt.

DOGS reading this will find these directions sound like normal behaviour. CATS may find it a stretch to even pretend they could be interested enough to do these things. CATS need to remember how necessary it is to foster DOGS in order to get their full support and achieve the objective. CATS need happy DOGS to support them and carry out the plan.

"Here, Gentlemen, a dog teaches us a lesson in humanity."
Napoleon Bonaparte

SUMMARY Checklist

'Approachable' Delivery to make DOGS comfortable:

- Use a melodious, rhythmical and varied tone of voice

- Lean forward, allow your head to tilt, smile more

- When speaking, bob your head naturally with the words.

- Stand asymmetrically, with your toes angled outwards.

- Shift weight to be more on one foot than the other.

- Use lots of gestures, especially with palms facing up.

N.B. Keep breathing low in abdomen to avoid sounding 'pleading'

"If animals could speak the dog would be a blundering outspoken fellow, but the cat would have the rare grace of never saying a word too much."
Mark Twain

Handling CATS

CATS stand out from the crowd. It's easy to spot CATS because these independent thinkers are often putting their attention elsewhere or making themselves the centre of attention. Smart leaders know they need to identify who the key CATS are and what drives them. Although CATS may seem arrogant, they are highly proactive, competitive, ambitious, and goal oriented. As natural inventors, they love dreaming up new ideas, brainstorming, exploring different options and making changes. They prefer the big picture overview rather than detail.

Full of confidence, CATS seek decision making positions of power. They'll never do anything unless they choose to do it themselves. They like working alone, being in command of their own territory. CATS are so comfortable with power that they make good leaders. They don't shy from conflict and actually enjoy provoking debates. Highly competitive, they can be stimulated into action through competing with the excellence of other CATS. But watch out, because they may be angling for your job!

CATS only respect other, higher CATS. They hardly notice the existence of anyone else (unless useful for their purpose). Unlike the friendly DOGS, a CAT can walk right past people without seeing or acknowledging them. They can appear cold or even dysfunctional. At meetings they may give little eye contact. During conversations, they may give you intense direct eye contact. If they stare you down, this may be an unconscious power play. The person who blinks or looks away first gives deference to the higher CAT. Compliments are meaningless to them - unless they come from someone in a higher position. CATS stay cool, calm and unflappable in the face of stress. But curiously, a CAT will explode for effect, if they think an emotional outburst will enhance their power play. But that's all for show, as they rarely feel upset.

"In a cat's eye, all things belong to cats."
English Proverb

Influencing CATS

If you respect CATS and admire their expertise, they may tolerate a 'fellowship of equals'. If you can tweak their curiosity, get them interested in a new, innovative development project, they might choose to get involved. Appealing to their higher values will help to motivate them. Motivate them even further by 'teasing' them. Instead of supplying full information about a project, give them tantalizing overviews and make them want to know more. CATS can also be motivated by competition and bonus reward schemes. When giving feedback, it's possible to be quite direct without creating offence.

Top Tip:

Key Factors to remember when dealing with CATS

1. Be prepared! Know your subject and your objective

2. Appeal to their values, drivers and motivators

3. Know the hierarchy and give appropriate deference

4. Tweak their curiosity, make them want to know more

5. Give them their own space & time to decide for themselves

6. Build and use the political network of the other key CATS

Keep it SIMPLE

Although there are times when CATS will demand to know all the details and relevant facts, they usually prefer to receive such information pre-digested and summarised succinctly. It's vital to avoid rambling, so choose only stories / examples that are most pertinent. Get to the point. Remember that CATS want to be impressed by your expertise and competence. When it comes to work, they are less interested in having friendly conversation. So, above all, be prepared for this meeting.

Many CATS speak in an abbreviated fashion, so it's good to match this when you want to be on their wavelength. You may have had the experience of launching into a diatribe of detail on some pet subject, only to have your CAT listener start looking bored, yawn, interrupt or make a rapid exit. Instead, you may want to shorten your sentences. Think 'John Wayne'. Although it may feel strange to do this at first, here's something to practice when talking to CATS:

Limit your message to 3 or 4 words: e.g.

I'll be there

Maybe you're right

Consider it done

You know the answer

Ask your heart

I made a mistake

I am sorry

The Power of SINCERE Apology

CATS as a rule don't apologise because nothing is ever their fault. They don't make mistakes. Even when mistakes happen, they focus on winning next time. DOGS apologise too much, even for things that are not their fault, hoping to win favour and maintain a good relationship. When a situation does demand an apology, make sure it is a genuine one and keep it brief. When a person says 'I'm sorry IF what I did made you feel 'X', that is not an apology. It places blame on the perceiver - it makes it his fault for having a mis-perception. This may cause offence. Instead, use a sincere voice tone and simply express your genuine apology (even if you didn't do anything wrong). 'I'm sorry that 'X' happened. It won't happen again.' Good leaders know that the more accountability they hold, the greater their responsibility and power.

To Have More INFLUENCE...

To Have More INFLUENCE ~ Act Like a CAT

In order to win the respect of CATS in the room, you need to increase the credibility in your voice tone, body posture and mannerisms. You will only hold the CATS attention, if what you say interests them. They want to be impressed by what you are offering. They want to admire you, not like you. Their attention is mainly on the issue/ project /outcome, not on the relationship. Expect them to look down at the document, or out the window, while they decide for themselves what to think. This does not mean they are not listening.

CATS will be motivated if you tell them how new ideas could change the whole company. Give messages clearly but not too thoroughly – keep the CAT wanting to know more. When speaking, pause longer, to give emphasis to important points. The longer you pause, the greater the perception of your intelligence. Remember CATS respect stillness and silence. Pausing will also increase your leadership potential with DOGS.

However, when speaking to a CAT in a higher position than you, be sure to give proper deference and respect. Coming on too strong and giving a direct stare may arouse their competitive nature. Never corner a CAT.

CAT Influencing Strategies

Traits such as productivity and efficiency are values desired by people who are credible, i.e. CATS. Leaders need to be competent, definitive, and willing. CATS enjoy a challenge.

- Know the chain of command and ask approval from appropriate parties.

- Obtain the hierarchical chart and a flow chart of the power.

- Know the company's values and refer to them in conversation.

- Be aware of different department's contributions and factually acknowledge them.

- Let people know consequences, give warnings, before rules are enforced.

- Be more formal in speech, dress and behaviours.

How to Sound More CREDIBLE

The following behaviours require practice! CATS speak in 'commands'. The sound of each sentence is loud, authoritative, and goes down at the end for emphasis. The most important characteristic to remember is to breathe low in your belly and slow. Then PAUSE more often, especially after an important piece of information [Silently count 1,2,3 during your pause]. Do NOT smile, do not blink or tilt your head. Keep a serious face and be 'still'. Close your mouth in between your sentences. Speak without any emotion in your voice - almost a monotone. Think Mr. Spock in Star Trek. Keep hand gestures to an absolute minimum and only move for emphasis. You've probably noticed CATS using this style at meetings. Perhaps you've also noticed when people do the opposite - how differently did you perceive their contribution?

If you already have predominant CAT tendencies, you may find this style familiar and easy. Are there situations where you could do this even more effectively? DOGS may find these behaviours feel quite awkward at first, un-natural and un-friendly. Remind yourself to focus on the higher objective of your message and know that showing more leadership will be good for increasing your INFLUENCE.

Checklist: Non-Verbals of INFLUENCE

- Use a flat voice tone with 'command' intonation curling down at the end of each sentence. Aim to sound definitive and confident.

- Pause after making your point to allow the importance to sink in. This gives listeners time to think and remember what you said.

- Keep your face and body still. Don't smile, don't nod or tilt your head.

- Stand with your weight equally on both feet, toes pointed straight ahead.

- Keep your arms either by your sides or at right angles, NOT in pockets or clasped below your waist, behind your back, or in a prayer position.

- Use few gestures, preferably with palms facing down.

N.B. Keep breathing low in the abdomen to avoid sounding angry

TWO: The Language of Influence

Looking and sounding credible, by using CAT strategies and body language, handles 93% of how your ideas will be perceived. Who you speak to and how you structure your talk will address the remaining 7%. First you need to identify who the key players are - those who will sway the decision making. If you succeed in winning their agreement, chances are that everyone else will follow. However, these key players may present resistance and opposition.

"Think twice before you speak, because your words and influence will plant the seed of either success or failure in the mind of another."
Napoleon Hill

OVERCOME Objections & Resistance

Have you ever wished you could make 'conscientious objectors' more open minded? Have you ever noticed that the more enthusiasm you show when presenting an idea, the more sceptical and resistant some people become? The more positive you sound, the less credible you seem to them. It's almost as if enthusiasm breeds scepticism. But you've probably also had successful interactions when you did manage to win people over. What made that work? Did you use reason, logic or strong argument to make them see the light? Did you tease, cajole, beg or plead? Different methods work at different times with different people. What if you could predict which style would work each time? The following outline is adapted from the work of communication expert Shelle Rose Charvet.

Presenting to SCEPTICS

The 4 Step Process for Presenting to Sceptics

Here's a great strategy for designing your message. Gandhi used to do something like this before every important meeting. The day before, he would set out chairs for each person who would attend the meeting and then sit in each chair pretending he was that person. He would carefully enter that person's world, thinking through their goals, what their objections might be, what motivated them and what hidden agenda they might have. Then he would construct his responses to each one. The next day at the meeting, he was able to answer every challenge eloquently with ease.

PRE-EMPT the Sceptics!

1. **What is the most important point or objective you want to get across?** What response do you want? Do you want agreement? A change of perspective? Some decision to be made? Action to be taken?

2. **Identify the form of resistance.** Consider each of the key people who will attend. What issues did they bring up last time? What objections might they have? What needs or agendas will occupy their focus? Re-assess your message from their perspective. Think of the most cynical, negative and sceptical forms of resistance they might use to challenge you.

3. **Decide how to handle each possible challenge.** Source well known evidence to prove your message holds true. List the reasons why they should accept and agree. What questions will allow people to reflect and decide for themselves? If you can, structure your response using the word 'because' in your sentences. The word 'because' helps deflect resistance.

4. **Open your message by cleverly pacing all possible objections.** Briefly introduce your topic. Using common experiences, address any possible resistance by thoroughly talking through all the objections BEFORE they come up. This takes the wind out of the sceptic's sails. Invite people to consider these common experiences, and always finish with a positive one. Then link your message to connect these problems with your solution. People will perceive you as being thorough in your thinking process. You will sound like you have taken into account all possible points of view.

Important Points about SCEPTICS

- They look at what is not possible
- They find exceptions - where it won't work
- They demand more and more proof
- They focus on problems, not goals
- They want to 'prevent' problems happening
- They don't want to be told what to think
- They need to evaluate for themselves
- They are unimpressed by name dropping
- They frequently change their minds
- They're so busy, time is very precious
- They don't want to be blamed for mistakes
- They'll dismiss you if your argument has flaws

Avoiding RESISTANCE

Special language for avoiding resistance

By using some key phrases, it is possible to deflect resistance and encourage consideration. Robert Cialdini, Ph.D in his book *'Influence: The Psychology of Persuasion'* talks about an experiment by Harvard social psychologist, Ellen Langer, that concluded people respond if they have a **reason** for what they do.

The experiment took place with people queuing up to use a photo copy machine. The experimenters would walk up and ask to queue jump. The first excuse they used was *'Excuse me, I have 5 pages. May I use the copy machine because I'm in a rush?'* This request coupled with a reason had a 94% success rate. Simply asking *'May I use the copy machine?'* had only 60% success. Surprisingly, simply saying *'Excuse me, I have five pages. May I use the machine because I have to make some copies?'* also got 93% success. Just using the word BECAUSE was enough to trigger most people into thinking there was a good reason, even when there wasn't.

USEFUL Phrases

Useful Phrases to Pace Resistance

This new concept/approach will work because.....

Here's an idea you may wish to consider....

Only you can decide if this won't work for you...

After you've had time to think this over, you can decide if it fits for you...

It's not my job to tell you what to think or how to do...

Only you know what is or isn't important...

With your experience and knowledge in this area...

The way I see it, your role is......and my role is... (equal but different)

Here are 'Ten Tips' for...(rather than 'Ten Rules')

The only way you'll know for sure is to try it out for yourself...

Don't believe me! Test it and see for yourself!

Apparently 'X' company had this issue, and what they did was....

What has worked to solve this problem before?

What to AVOID

Telling people what to think or what to choose often guarantees rejection. People resist being told something in a directive manner. They want to think for themselves and make up their own mind. Whenever you invite people to do this, you are likely to encourage a much better response.

Remember that big CATS have attitude. They don't have problems - problems are due to other people's making. They know everything and are more important than everyone else. Therefore you need to avoid implying anything that could offend in both spoken or written communication:

- Don't suggest there is something they don't already know

- Don't tell them what to think, choose or do

- Don't imply they have a problem and you have the solution

- Don't hint that they are not perfect in some way

- Don't imply you are better than they are in some way

"Don't tell people how to do things,
tell them what to do and let them surprise you with their results."
George S. Patton

Top tip:
Always think to yourself: If I say this, how might it be perceived by the other person looking at this situation through their eyes? How might this affect our relationship?

The object of using more careful phrasing is to get people to adopt a mental and emotional state of openness, where they will be able to HEAR what you are saying. When you are successful at getting people to listen and take you seriously, it's because you have cleared enough mental space in the other person for your words to be heard.

EXAMPLE

Presuppositions

A Sales Director with a rather driven, aggressive and competitive attitude did not notice the effect he had on his team. His rather controlling beliefs about action and meeting targets damaged the atmosphere of the whole department. Fear and competition had led to a very low level of trust and co-operation. As he wasn't aware of the atmosphere he created, confronting him directly would not work.

So with some positive presuppositions from NLP in mind: 'Everyone has all the resources they need; There's a positive intention behind every behaviour; There's no such thing as failure only feedback: Mistakes are learning opportunities when viewed correctly; The most flexible person will have the most influence and control of the system' I began to ask him questions just to open up his thinking and help him be more flexible in his approach.

After listening to his description of events, I chose my words carefully. I simply said, 'When observing different companies, it's easy for me to notice the different energy and atmosphere that is created by how people work together. From what you say, there isn't much co-operation or communication going on in your department. I wonder why no one on your team dares to talk about what's important?' This question led to us exploring why there was a lack of trust, and why people didn't feel safe enough to openly communicate. Without directly confronting him, it was possible to then suggest ways he could improve the situation by changing his manner.

DEATHLY Silence

Perhaps you've attended a meeting where the boss presents a completely unrealistic suggestion and no one says a word. Everyone tries to ignore this white elephant, pretending it's not there. No one speaks up. They are afraid to speak because on previous occasions, any voice of reason was quickly squashed, rejected or vetoed. No one dares to risk confrontation for fear of further humiliation and loss of favour. Most people prefer to avoid conflicts and deal with issues privately. So a deadly silence ensues.

According to Susan Scott, author of 'Fierce Conversations', an influential leader must avoid this tendency for people to maintain such polite silence. Real communication and participation must be encouraged. Otherwise, people will try to work around the white elephant to avoid causing offence, hoping it will go away. Communication declines, respect, trust and co-operation diminish, time is wasted, performance deteriorates, and ultimately, productivity is at risk. Over time, the loss of respect causes disillusionment and dissatisfaction which may lead to loss of top talent. To avert this, the leader needs to encourage the powerful silence of listening.

"Never mistake talking for conversation.
Anyone can play the notes,
the magic is in the intervals, in the phrasing."
Susan Scott

Powerful Silence = LISTENING

Inspired leadership draws on the talent, wisdom and diversity of other people. No one person has all the answers. When the stakes are high, emotions run strong. That's the crucial time for a leader to handle hotly opposing viewpoints and listen. The way these crucial conversations are managed is the most reliable indicator of organisational effectiveness. A successful solution can only be discovered through encouraging the free-flow of information, honest feedback and then brain storming new ideas.

CATS & DOGS both fall into traps when the stakes are high. DOGS jump into 'fix it' mode and think they must come up with all the solutions and present 'fait accompli' decisions. CATS may believe they need to impress everyone with their brilliance, so they talk too much instead of listening. Both think they must have the answer for every problem. Instead of benefiting from the insight, creativity and genius of others, the same old decisions and mistakes get repeated. Rather than talking so fast, filling the air space, and making lots of noise, the leader needs to recognise that active silence creates the space for the right answers to surface.

Encourage silence whenever someone:

- Tends to monopolise the airspace
- Interrupts or talks over the speaker
- Plans what to say next while others talk
- Responds too quickly with little or no thought
- Tries too hard to be clever, impressive or likeable
- Jumps in with fix it advice or solutions too soon
- Seizes any pause or break to change topics
- Waffles instead of saying something constructive

"There can be no power without mystery. There must always be a 'something' which others cannot altogether fathom, which puzzles them, stirs them, and rivets their attention.... Nothing more enhances authority than silence. It is the crowning virtue of the strong, the refuge of the weak, the modesty of the proud, the pride of the humble, the prudence of the wise, and the sense of fools."
Charles de Gaulle

CRUCIAL Conversations

Crucial Conversations: How to Invite Contribution

When a leader needs to encourage participation, what works best is to ask powerful questions and then pause, creating a vacuum of silence to suck in contributions, new thinking and creative participation. People need to feel heard. If their ideas are taken seriously, then they feel such input makes a difference. Of course, attributing credit to the right person for a valuable contribution encourages this process too. Remember that DOGS particularly believe everyone's opinion counts. So it is essential that everyone is listened to and appreciated. When you want to keep key CATS on board, treat them as a 'fellowship of equals', and listen respectfully.

Top Tip:

When inviting people to voice their opinions or challenge a proposal, the leader must resist the urge to defend or argue. Resist this natural temptation because it unwittingly gives the message that the leader knows best. This stifles participation. Listen and gather alternative views instead.

"The conversation is not about the relationship.
The conversation IS the relationship."
Susan Scott

DIRECT Questions

Ask Direct Questions, Add Silence and Shake

Before tackling an important conversation, it's crucial to separate the people from the problem and to set aside the judgements, conclusions or stories that you may have already convinced yourself are true. Instead, ask yourself 'Why would a reasonable, intelligent & experienced person think, say or do this?' Be curious. Assuming most people work with positive intentions in mind goes a long way to increasing understanding. That doesn't mean they are right, just that they thought they were doing the right thing according to their map of the world. You can only find out by asking. But assuming a positive intent helps.

Top Tip:
Your communication = what the other person understands and takes away

An influential leader interrogates all key players to discover each different version of reality. The objective is to provoke learning, tackle the real issues and maintain relationships. Whenever you ask direct questions, you must make it clear that you are inviting dialogue by leaving enough silence to encourage people to offer their opinions, disagree with you and present their facts. Couple this with 'palm up' open gestures that invite participation for best results. Resist jumping to defend your views. Listen and gather information thoroughly. Summarise and paraphrase what they say to make sure you've heard correctly.

OUTCOME Frame

Crucial Conversation Outcome Frame

1. What is the crux of the present state situation?

2. What impact has this had on me, on others, on results, etc.?

3. If this continues, what are the consequences? What's at stake?

4. How have I contributed to this situation? How have others contributed?

5. What ideal and specific Win/Win outcome could work better?

6. When this issue is resolved, what evidence will be the measure?

7. What resources are needed and who needs to be involved?

8. What obstacles could get in the way and how can they be dealt with?

9. What are the first 3 steps towards achieving this resolution?

10. What specifically is each person committed to do and by when?

Getting the WRONG End of the Stick

Most people have had the experience of being misinterpreted or misunderstood. Suppose you say something and your listener gets upset. From their perspective, they had a reason to get upset and a reason to defend, dismiss, resist or reject what you were saying. So if you really want to get your point across, and you start to notice some kind of negative reaction to your message, it helps to stop and say, *'Wait a minute, that's not what I meant. Let me re-phrase that. It certainly wasn't my intention to upset you.'* Then restate your message until it is clearly understood the way you meant it.

"When you can do nothing, what can you do?
When you don't know, what would it be if you did know?"
Zen Koan

THREE: Positive Politics

Alliance with the right network

Most people cringe when the subject of politics is mentioned. It usually goes unspoken, denied, avoided or dreaded because of negative associations. Many people have had their enthusiasm squashed by coming up against the existence of invisible walls: decisions being made behind the scenes, meetings held where it is obvious that conclusions have already been drawn, messages being ignored, and alliances that seem to favour certain individuals. Such politics often offend people's values.

In order to truly have influence, a leader needs to understand and manage organisational politics. The most powerful people may not hold high positions in the hierarchy. Even though people try to deny its presence, political behaviour is present in almost every organisation. So it would be naïve to ignore it. Politics can have a major impact on career advancement, stress levels, motivation and productivity. It can even affect customer relationships and satisfaction, thereby diminishing revenue. How can a leader avoid the downward spiral of mistrust and intrigue that can create such harm?

Whether political behaviour is seen as positive or manipulative depends on the perception of the observer. Lobbying for support before presenting a new project at a meeting could be seen as manipulative by some. Whilst others may consider doing that a perfectly legitimate and intelligent way of informing key people. When time is short, and competition for money or resources is high, expect a great deal more political manoeuvring to occur. You may have already guessed that CATS are naturally better at managing politics than DOGS.

Getting Things DONE

A more positive perspective might be to view politics as a way to get things done by using informal channels. Leaders need to be able to quickly recognise key people and make sure they are on board, because the rest will follow. It is much easier to explain complex issues and get agreement one-to-one than it is to present perfectly to a group, hoping they will all listen and understand and agree with the points you make. Private discussion meetings ahead of time can often be a totally sensible and informal way to operate. When you appreciate that most of the key people will be CATS, and that each CAT has a tough attitude that can be very difficult to convince, it's easy to understand why organisational politics will never go away. If a particular CAT who will attend the meeting, could squash the open consideration of a proposal, then having a prior discussion to discover their objections might be wise.

"I must follow the people.
Am I not their leader?"
Benjamin Disraeli

EXERCISE

How Politically Savvy are You?

Score the following statements 1 - 10 as to how true they are for you.

1. Playing politics can dangerously risk
your relationships and career 1 2 3 4 5 6 7 8 9 10

2. It's important to understand who and
where the power is in the organisation ... 1 2 3 4 5 6 7 8 9 10

3. Reason, facts, thorough presentations
and open debate should always win. 1 2 3 4 5 6 7 8 9 10

4. There are many long term benefits
from developing allies and networks. 1 2 3 4 5 6 7 8 9 10

5. Meeting my job description & satisfying
my direct report is what I'm here to do. .. 1 2 3 4 5 6 7 8 9 10

6. If I've done favours for others, I'm
comfortable asking for favours in return. 1 2 3 4 5 6 7 8 9 10

7. Difficult issues and problems should
always be dealt with immediately. 1 2 3 4 5 6 7 8 9 10

8. Total openness may not be
appropriate in all situations..................... 1 2 3 4 5 6 7 8 9 10

9. No one should get special treatment
or be favoured. 1 2 3 4 5 6 7 8 9 10

10. It's important to pick the right time &
place to deal with difficult issues. 1 2 3 4 5 6 7 8 9 10

11. Networking is unnecessary if everyone
openly co-operates & works together. 1 2 3 4 5 6 7 8 9 10

12. It's not what you know, it's who you
know that counts. 1 2 3 4 5 6 7 8 9 10

13. The most important projects should
always get the necessary budget. 1 2 3 4 5 6 7 8 9 10

14. Effective networking is a critical factor
for success in business. 1 2 3 4 5 6 7 8 9 10

15. Total openness and honesty is always
the best approach.................................... 1 2 3 4 5 6 7 8 9 10

16. Because resources are always limited,
it's necessary to use influence. 1 2 3 4 5 6 7 8 9 10

17. Politics is a unnecessary power game
for ambitious people. 1   2   3   4   5   6   7   8   9   10

18. Managing politics is crucial to the
success of the organisation. 1   2   3   4   5   6   7   8   9   10

19. Friendly relationships and loyal
camaraderie are what I seek and trust... 1   2   3   4   5   6   7   8   9   10

20. I can trust anyone, even an enemy, as
long as the objectives are compatible 1   2   3   4   5   6   7   8   9   10

Total your scores for EVEN and ODD numbered statements.

Your ODD number score indicates how much DOG attitude you might have. This
may indicate lower political savvy, although you may have lots of friends. If this
score is high, you might benefit from considering some new perspectives about
influence and impact, and how to get key people on board.

Your EVEN number score indicates how much CAT attitude you have. A high
score may indicate higher political savvy and more influencing ability. Be sure to
remember to take care of all the people in your department.

If your scores were more or less equal, then you have the best possible
combination for acting as a liaison or developing inspired leadership capacity. You
have the ability to reach all the people.

Common RESPONSES to Politics

According to research on political awareness done by psychologists Simon Baddeley and Kim James, people react in 4 different ways to politics. The first type [Sheep] refuses to accept that politics exist, a somewhat innocent and naïve attitude. The second type [Donkeys] believe they know everything about politics when they don't and then go about stubbornly pursuing their goals whilst deluding themselves. The third type [Foxes] use charm, cunning, and exploit devious ways to use the system for personal gain. The fourth type [Owls] have high awareness and wield expert political skill to achieve win/win organisational and personal goals.

Sheep risk being ignored unless they become more politically aware. Donkeys need to become more aware of what is really going on. Foxes are probably responsible for the bad perception of politics. They may be mistrusted for their selfish motives, but they can learn to work with others for the good of the organisation. Owls stay vigilant because they know there's always room for improvement. Influential leaders need to develop Owl characteristics.

"Position yourself as a centre of influence -
the one who knows the movers and shakers.
People will respond to that, and you'll soon
become what you project."
Bob Burg

SIX Useful Tools

Six Useful Tools for Positive Politics

#1 Key Political Tool = Communication

Influence and impact depend on a leader's ability to speak the language of the listeners. By quickly identifying whether the audience shows CAT or DOG tendencies, a leader can instantly adapt how the message needs to be delivered. For example, the CATS may respond better to succinct summaries, whilst the DOGS may prefer to hear all the details to make sure you've covered everything in depth and avoided all the pitfalls. The CATS will get excited by something new, different, and innovative with lots of options. The DOGS will relax when they know each alternative has been carefully researched and not too many trusted procedures will need to change. Once you appreciate fully how the inner thinking of CATS & DOGS pervades all communication, your ability to politically adjust how you present your message will soar.

Top Tip:
Make sure you thoroughly understand a person's position: their objectives, motivations, agendas, and reservations before making them an ally.

"Hell, there are no rules here -
we're trying to accomplish something."
Thomas A. Edison

#2 Key Political Tool = Trust

Most people expect trust to happen automatically as a result of appropriate behaviour, but they may be less aware that certain actions enhance or detract from the perception of being trustworthy. Some people inadvertently use poor habits of communication that block trust from developing. Encouraging comparison or competition between members of a team often breeds separation. Favouritism leads to resentment and exclusion. The right kind of openness and inclusiveness creates trust. Trust creates effective relationships. Effective relationships make great allies. Allies help you to achieve objectives.

"To lead people, walk beside them ...
As for the best leaders, the people do not notice their existence.
The next best, the people honor and praise.
The next, the people fear;
and the next, the people hate ...
When the best leader's work is done the people say,
'We did it ourselves!'"

Lao-tsu

Simple ways to increase Trust:

1. Use open questions to encourage communication.

2. Be quiet and listen, get all the facts and how they feel.

3. Clarify and paraphrase what they say to check understanding.

4. Avoid leading questions that attempt to win premature agreement.

5. Tell people 'why' you need to know the answer to your question.

6. Be open about potential implications or responsibilities.

7. Keep aware of information coming through the grapevine.

8. Share information, divulge facts & figures whenever appropriate.

9. Think aloud so that others can follow your line of reasoning.

10. Follow through on what you say you'll do.
Be true to your word.

#3 Key Political Tool = Play to Your Strengths

Each person has unique abilities, talents and skills, but there's a natural tendency to lose sight of those when a challenging situation triggers feelings of inadequacy. There's a temptation to compare yourself with someone of brilliance and think you have to be like that instead of making the most of what you have to offer. So it pays to think carefully and list what all your strengths are, so that it's easy to draw on them when needed. A leader who recognises and acknowledges the unique contributions of each individual empowers everyone to give their best. Here's a sample list of some positive qualities.

What are your strengths?

- Reputation for effective action
- An eye for detail, thoroughness
- Special experience or expertise
- High integrity, trustworthy
- Fast speed of response
- Great people skills
- Access to the budget
- Being proactive, positive
- Being creative, innovative
- Useful network of contacts
- Technological capability
- Effective team backup
- Dynamic presentations

"The trouble is, if you don't risk anything, you risk even more."
Erica Jong

#4 Key Political Tool = Your Network

Mention networking to some people and they groan because they think it means going out to glad hand strangers at events and make trivial conversation. Influential leaders know differently. A network starts with your one-to-one relationships as well as more formal business meetings. It includes meeting people where you socialise, do sports, holiday or relax. If you attend discussion groups, clubs, conferences, professional associations, talks or training events, you can meet and develop contacts anywhere.

Different people have different styles. Some 'work the room' and try to meet as many people as possible, whilst others focus on the ones that interest them the most. The quality - not quantity - of your network has a direct and profound effect on how influential and successful you become.

Think about who is already a part of your network. Think about all the people you currently interact with. Then consider, in light of your own personal objectives and career interests, who might be the most useful contacts to have? Where could you easily cross paths with such people on a regular basis? What activities can you schedule in your diary? What associations, conferences, societies, groups or other interests could you join?

"The successful networkers I know, the ones receiving tons of referrals and feeling truly happy about themselves, continually put the other person's needs ahead of their own."
Bob Burg

How well are you keeping up with the people you already
know? A network is only useful if it is kept active and updated.
If you haven't spoken to someone for many years, not only will
their address have changed but their personal circumstances
may also be different. Schedule time to check in with the
important people on your network regularly in order to maintain
the relationship.

#5 Key Political Tool = Being Known

Influential leaders do not lurk in the shadows hoping someone will notice them. They show up and step forward, letting people see and get to know them. Without being arrogant or pompous, an influential leader just naturally takes a genuine interest in getting to know others, their issues, problems, needs and concerns, in order to create good relationships. Because they listen well, they're good at remembering specific things that have been said. They are also quick to recognise and applaud the success of others.

Being known is as important on the small scale as the large scale. How helpful might it be to develop a great relationship with your Boss's PA? What if you supported and mentored promising new recruits who thank you later on for helping them to success? What if you developed a great reputation as a team player? What if you volunteered for project teams, task forces or working parties? How about writing articles, giving talks or participating in other events? Brainstorm some appropriate places where you could show up and be seen.

"The only real training for leadership is leadership. "
Antony Jay

#6 Key Political Tool = Positive Mental Attitude

It's very rare to find a good leader that has a 'glass half empty' attitude. Being positive and upbeat is simply more attractive and compelling. Instead of focusing on problems, what's not working, and what could go wrong, influential leaders carefully balance their communication. When they do present a problem, they also suggest potential solutions as well as seeking others input. They stay focused on the positive vision and reframe any problems as merely temporary challenges.

Influential leaders master the genuine Win/Win attitude. Not I win, and then I win again. They avoid compromise where accepting solutions means no one is satisfied. They know 'follow through' is as important as intention. While respecting that timing can be a crucial factor, they intuit when it's appropriate to be flexible. They are willing to take unpopular decisions, accept the flak and take responsibility for mistakes. They learn from each mistake and forgive others when mistakes are made.

"When the effective leader is finished with his work, the people say it happened naturally."
Lao Tse

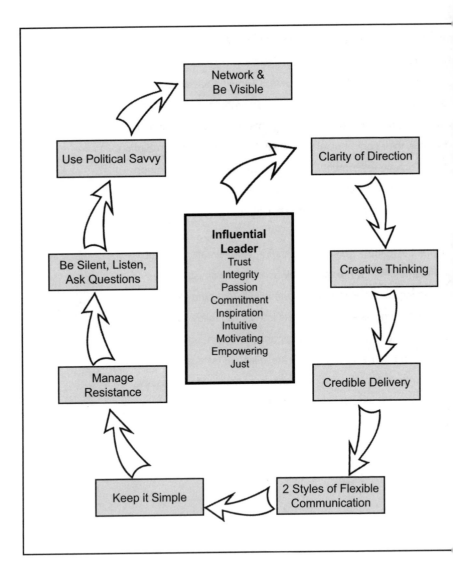

SUMMARY

Influence and impact begin with having clarity of direction. Being positive, proactive, credible and confident inspires people to want to follow. Great leaders show genuine interest in others, encouraging co-operation and teamwork, gathering everyone's input in order to make maximum use of available talent. They have an open and giving attitude. New ideas, innovative thinking and creative solutions are valued. They communicate clearly and simply, varying their style according to who they are talking to and listening carefully to what is said. They've mastered the knack of asking pertinent questions. Their use of silence invites participation. Such influential leaders have developed useful networks and manage their power informally, with respect to the political structure. They exude quiet authority, with a natural and genuine demeanour.

A Plum Job

Motivating Your People during Times of Change

by Rose Padfield

MOTIVATING Your People

Pace and Speed of Change

The pace of life has increased dramatically in recent years. Who has not had a conversation about the speed of change and how we are all expected to do more with less? Life is less predictable, more complex and much, much faster.

Consumers have more choice, and suppliers have more competition. Thanks to information technology, consumers respond instantly to new market trends. Customer demands mean that companies must respond with cheaper, better, cleverer products.

Customer expectations of customer service soar. Take, for example, the UK pharmaceutical industry. Patients can now access knowledge about a drug from the Internet at the touch of a button. They demand the best-in-class medicine from an increasingly cost-constrained health service. Consumers shop around and companies have to race to keep up.

The Internet and other technological tools mean that there is a raised expectation about communication – everyone is contactable 24/7. An internal paper memo used to take a whole day to reach your desk, whereas today it's instantaneous. So is it surprising that response times are expected to be the same? Added to the pressure of faster deadlines, increased competition from abroad, cost cutting, the stress of mergers and acquisitions, and the menu of difficulties that a leader faces today can seem daunting.

An effective leader must intuit the right vision, and then he or she needs to bring everyone along with them. They must know how to motivate and influence without being controlling and dominating. They need to make an immediate impact, provide a speedy response and keep up-to-date with current trends.

The atmosphere of the work environment has changed too. Open plan offices, flat hierarchical structures and geographically dispersed teams have all led to a need for a different kind of leader. The old dominating, controlling, authoritarian, dogmatic style of leadership has become obsolete. What works today are leaders who can win the respect of their teams and colleagues, who can motivate and influence with integrity, bearing in mind that different situations and individuals require different motivating styles.

This chapter gives you tips and exercises to help improve job satisfaction for you and your teams – because when you're all working at optimum effectiveness, productivity improves.

"Nothing is permanent but change."
Heraclitus

SHIFTING sands

The contract between employee and employer has shifted in the last 15 years. Before, security and length of service were valued. Now, employees expect:

- a meaningful role
- practical help with their lifestyle
- to feel personally engaged with the company

As fierce competition for top quality employees continues, employers must evolve their working practices to attract, develop and retain their talent. Those organisations who have addressed these needs have the edge.

Examples of New Working Practices

- Some employers offer a concierge service to help employees with their domestic requirements, reducing conflict between work and home (and of course enabling them to be more available at work).

- Companies who now conduct personalised marketing to employees to excite them and connect with them around the vision and goals.

- Other lifestyle support such as on-site health facilities, as well as access to telephone helplines for family support.

EXAMPLE

Innocent Drinks

Innocent Drinks make pure fruit smoothies with no additives. Their brand has a quirky humour that's consistent throughout all their marketing, including their website, newsletter, blog and even their packaging. They've been awarded awarded The Best Workplace in the UK by The Guardian and The National Business Awards.

As well as share options, a healthcare plan, a £2,000 bonus on having a baby and the chance to receive a £1,000 scholarship to pursue outside interests, employees have a range of after-hours clubs to choose from, including the cheese club. Innocent also promote their ethical and environmental standards such as through their registered charity, the Innocent Foundation, which invests 10% of their profits in the countries where they buy their fruit, and by being first to introduce 100% recycled bottles.

A few of Innocent's other innovations include:
- Workplace entitled 'Fruit Towers'
- Floor covered in fake grass
- Phones answered "Hello, banana phone!"
- 'Dancing' delivery vans covered in grass or painted with cow designs, plus eyelashes, udders and horns
- 'Fruitstock' music festival and village fete
- 'The Big Knit' in conjunction with Sainsbury's (Customers knit woolly hats for the bottles. For each hat 50p is contributed to Age Concern to help keep old people warm in winter.)
- A tree planted for every carton registered

CHANGING your Perspective

So how do successful leaders motivate their people these days?

The starting point is to take time to understand where the other person is coming from: What motivates them? What do they want? How can you help them achieve their needs and aspirations? Leaders who value the importance of these insights are significantly more likely to have high performing teams consisting of individuals who feel valued and appreciated. Yet this is often a skill lacking even in senior leaders, who can be so focused on the business result that they forget to bring people with them. They may make progress initially but in the long run, the job satisfaction and productivity of their team may suffer.

Once you have a clear view of the other person's perspective you can build this into your understanding of the full context of the situation, such as the business climate and the outcome you want to achieve.

PUSH and PULL

Broadly speaking there are two styles of motivational behaviour – pull and push. With pull, the leader will bring people towards him or her through a style of collaboration and win-win. It may take longer to craft a solution but can be very motivating as everyone buys into the result. With push, the leader is likely to be more assertive and state what is expected, with people being required to comply. This style can be effective when a business is in crisis and strong, authoritative leadership is required. In the longer term and if consistently used it is unlikely to be effective at motivating and gaining commitment – particularly with today's employer-employee relationship.

EXAMPLE

Push v Pull

There is a popular Æsop fable that beautifully sums this up.

One day the wind and the sun were talking and observing a man walking along wearing a coat. The wind was boasting to the sun that he was stronger than the sun, and the sun was boasting to the wind that he was the strongest. So they decided to hold a competition: to see which of them could get the man to take off his coat. The wind started first. He blew his strongest and fiercest and was very powerful. The man obviously felt the wind but it did not blow his coat off – he drew it tightly around his body to protect himself from its power. Eventually the wind admitted defeat and let the sun have a go. So the sun came out and shone his strongest and sunniest. The warmth of his rays came through and created a lovely sunny day. The man showed his face up to the sun, closed his eyes and smiled as he appreciated the sun's warmth. He soon became too warm, and took his coat off. The wind admitted that his fierce power had not worked in this instance and reluctantly admitted defeat.

Bringing this into a business context, we all know leaders who are like the sun and we all know leaders who are like the wind. Depending on the situation it may be more effective to be like the wind and it may be more effective to be like the sun. Again, it is important to understand the situation and make a conscious choice as to which will be more effective.

Leadership RELATIONSHIPS

Creating a Leadership Template

The number one reason why people leave a company is due to the relationship with their boss. People value feeling they are part of a cohesive, succesful team where everybody is working together, where each person feels respected and valued for their contribution. This is more important to most people than how much money they earn!

It is essential for a leader to understand how to create the optimal working relationship with all direct reports. Although this will be different with each person to some extent, it will always incorporate the same key elements.

These key elements include:

- Trust
- Respect
- Time – giving time when it's needed
- Listening
- Sharing thoughts, ideas and feelings – being open
- Being receptive to a different point of view

Treating People as ADULTS

A situation that often comes up in coaching is when a leader treats people as children rather than as adults and the people respond as children, as explained in the model of Transactional Analysis. Before expanding on this theory further, the fundamentals behind TA are explained below, in an extract from the book "TA Today" by Ian Stewart and Vann Jones:

"The most fundamental assumption of TA is that people are OK. This means: you and I both have worth, value and dignity as people. I accept myself as me and I accept you as you. This is a statement of essence rather than behaviour.

At times, I may not like nor accept what you do. But always, I accept what you are. Your essence as a human being is OK with me, even though your behaviour may not be.

I am not one-up to you, and you are not one-up to me. We are on a level as people. This is true even though our accomplishments may differ. It is true even though we may be of different race, age or religion."

The theory of Transactional Analysis can be summarised as people adopting the role of Parent, Adult or Child. The optimal style to adopt is usually adult. Often however, the leader may adopt the role of Parent and overly direct, control and effectively bully the subordinate. The subordinate often adopts the role of Child in response, either by complying or rebelling. Alternatively the subordinate can still respond in Child but in a playful way to try and soften up the Parent leader, much as an indulgent parent will "let off" a naughty child.

Each individual has the power to choose how they behave and respond to situations, and has the responsibility to decide for themselves.

EXAMPLE

Parent : Child

John, a senior technical specialist, was suffering due to the behaviour of his boss, Fred, a Board member in a large global company. Fred was acting out critical Parent behaviour, such as criticising work, never being available to discuss matters, shouting, never praising, and overly controlling the work of the specialist. John was responding in typical Child behaviour and was afraid to openly confront the issues for fear of being fired. He lost confidence and became very closed towards colleagues. Towards his own people John behaved as Fred did towards him and overly dominated, ignored etc.

Exploring this model with John enabled him to change his behaviour to the role of Adult. By doing this he became calmer, more friendly and open towards colleagues and subordinates. He tackled the issue with Fred and they agreed more adult ways of working together. Their style of working became more respectful and open which in TA terms looks like: "I'm OK: You're OK".

Giving POSITIVE Feedback

Many people respond better to praise than to criticism. Here are three techniques that may help when giving appraisals or wishing to achieve a desired change in someone else's behaviour.

1. Give your negative feedback wrapped in a 'positive sandwich'. First, say something that you appreciate about them, then the thing you'd like them to change in future, and end with something else that's good about their contribution.

"It's great that you ... Next time, I'd like you to ... Your work was excellent on..."

2. Always comment on the person's behaviour, not on the person themselves. State how it makes you feel.

"I feel disappointed when you...because...What I'd prefer is..."

3. Agree in advance that you are each going to think of three things that you want to Start-Stop-Continue. Say something you want them to start doing, something you want them to stop doing, and something you want them to continue doing in the future. Also invite them to use the same technique with you in return (and be prepared to respond appropriately).

"I'd like you to start..."
"I'd like you to stop..."
"I'd like you to continue..."

EXERCISE

Part A – Being Your Best

Find a quiet place that allows for true and relaxed reflection, or if it's easier, find someone you trust to talk to – whichever style best suits you and helps you reflect.

As the leader of your team, think of a time when you were at your very best, a specific time that you excelled. What were you like - how would you describe it? What did you look like, sound like and what/how did you feel? What did you say to yourself? What enabled you to be like this? What did you believe? Where was your focus? What do you think worked so well? Why? Where else might these attributes be useful?

Part B – The Team's Experience

Now ask your team what it was like to be on the receiving end of this style of leadership. What did the individual team members see, hear and feel? How did they perceive you? What was the impact on the work and productivity as a result of this?

You can either choose to do this in one group or 1-1; whichever will give you the most honest feedback.

Part C – Compare and Contrast

Compare the results – both in terms of results and also the similarities and differences amongst the team members. Notice this and make a note of any key points and surprises.

This exercise will help you get to know yourself better and to become more conscious of what your natural strengths are. By checking with the team you'll build a picture of why it has worked for them, and learn the differences in what motivates others. Seeing these differences and being able to adapt your natural style to meet people in their "map of the world" is key in being able to motivate and influence – if you make it easy for others it greatly helps them give of their best.

"Leaders in the new organisation do not lack motivational tools, but the tools are different from those of traditional corporate bureaucrats. The new rewards are based not on status but on contribution, and they consist not of regular promotion and automatic pay rises but of excitement about mission and a share of the glory and the gains of success."
Rosabeth Moss Kanter, US academic, management author (b.1943)

EXERCISE

Part D – Experiencing your boss

The boss/subordinate relationship comes up time and time again in coaching and has an impact both on performance and self esteem. You may be a 'boss' to some people, but you are probably also a 'subordinate' to someone else. 'Managing upwards' is a useful skill to learn. If done well, it can create a happier working life and even help you get recognition and move up the career ladder.

Step outside the role of being the leader for a while, and reflect what it is like being on the receiving end of leadership yourself.

What does your boss do well and what is the impact on you, both in terms of how you feel and also your work productivity? What would you like him/her to do differently? What would you like him/her to start or stop doing?

Again, this exercise further increases your understanding of yourself and what your own needs are. By knowing what you need, you have more chance of ensuring these needs are met and so creating the optimal environment for yourself. It's also good practice to 'see the other side' and recognise how easy it is for a boss to influence you either positively or negatively.

EXAMPLE

Win win

Jane's employers were keen on providing personal development for their people, including psychological personality profiling. She developed a keen sense of personal insight and the ability to express her wants and needs.

She was able to discuss the results with her immediate boss and explain: 'This is the best way to manage me and get the best work out of me'.

Her boss was flexible enough to adapt to Jane's preferred style of management, and they developed a mutually happy and productive working relationship that lasted for years.

"The worst mistake a boss can make is not to say 'well done'."
John Ashcroft, former chairman, Coloroll

GET Started

So how can you create the most productive and empowering work environment? If feeling mutually respected as part of a highly motivated team is what people want, how can you build such teams?

The most productive environments often have these traits:

- Individuals can say what they think, when they think it
- People are allowed – even encouraged - to take initiative and risks
- People learn from mistakes rather than being blamed for them
- Individuals are given opportunities before they are 100% ready for them, and fully supported
- Praise is freely and fully given, and more so than criticism.

EXERCISE

Motivating the team

Metaphorically step inside the shoes of each member of the team – each person one at a time.

Ask yourself what motivates them. (It may help to literally sit in a different chair or stand in a separate space that represents each of your team in turn.) When you arrive at a conclusion, ask yourself how do you know this?

Prepare to be surprised by how much you can intuit by sincerely stepping into the shoes of someone else. Then test your theories by asking them: and notice the impact when you ask and **truly** listen to the response (with an open mind). Leaders in business often feel they need to know the answer and that asking questions demonstrates weakness – in fact the opposite is true.

This will provide you with more conscious information about how to lead the individuals within your team. It may throw up some surprising answers, not least in the variety of responses from individuals.

EXAMPLE

Motivating the team

Andrew was managing a project comprising individuals from diverse functions and geographies. None of them reported to him, but he was leading the project. He was struggling to inject some enthusiasm into the team and influence them to complete their tasks.

Together with his coach, he explored the differences in style of the team members and it was enlightening to him to discover the variance. He was a very task-driven individual and motivated by deadlines. He accomplished high volumes of work, in a serious methodical manner. To some individuals in the team this was stifling as they needed a more informal, creative environment where themes were debated rather than tasks.

By being more flexible in his style and method of communicating, the team became more motivated to accomplish their commitments and support each other.

INDIVIDUAL Differences

When working with teams, Myers Briggs is an effective tool for helping team members to understand difference, and to appreciate the value of that difference. Key questions to ask:

What value do I bring to this team?
What do I need from the others to complement this value?
What do I value in others?

So for example, using the Myers Briggs model of Extrovert and Introvert, the Extroverts often value the fact that Introverts will listen and then succinctly summarise the debate. The Introverts value the debate that Extroverts drive.

Another fun example to show the difference between individuals who are good at focusing on detail (Sensing types in Myers Briggs language) versus big picture individuals (Intuitive types in Myers Briggs language) is an exercise using a Salvador Dali poster. Simply hold up the poster and ask what people notice; the Sensing types will notice all the intricacies and small details of the poster, and the Intuitive types are more likely to notice the overview of the picture and try and understand its meaning. Bringing this example into a work context should show the value of both of these and that one without the other is not as effective as both together.

Finally, developing a Team Charter (or whatever term means the most to the team) creates a sense of how the team wish to work together, and the values/behaviours they agree on. The following exercise can help to develop this and is great for new teams or existing teams.

EXERCISE

Creating a Team Charter

First divide the team into three groups, to encourage creativity and participation by all. Take three pieces of flip chart paper and display them in different corners of the room. Head each flip chart paper with one of the following statements:

- What Has Never Worked and Now It's Time to Leave Behind

- What Has Worked for us in the Past and Now It's Time to Leave Behind

- What Works for us now and we Wish to Retain

Step 1:
Each group walks up to one flip chart stand, discusses the heading and writes in bullet point format what they believe in relation to the question. Allow approximately 5-10 minutes.

Step 2:
Then each group moves round one so that they are standing at the next flip chart. They review what's there and add bullet points as they see fit – they do not change what has been written there already.

Step 3:
Finally, after a further 5-10 minutes they move to the last flip chart stand and repeat Step 2.

Once all three groups have completed each flip chart the original group in Step 1 presents to the rest of the team what they have written and why. Each group does the same for their original flip chart.

The group discuss and agree (whilst respecting everyone's views and the fact that there will be difference).

The final step is to then build on the third flipchart – What Works for us now and we Wish to Retain – and add new behaviours/values so that this becomes the Charter.

To conclude the exercise the group can decide what they wish to do with the other flip charts: to honour what has worked well in the past but is now no longer appropriate going forward; and to "bury" what has never worked well.

With the agreed charter it's a good idea to have a creative person in the team to create a memento to keep it alive – perhaps laminate into A5 for each individual, or create a coaster with it. The newly created charter could also be visibly displayed in the office and/or at meetings.

> *"Freedom is not worth having*
> *if it does not include the freedom to make mistakes."*
> *Mahatma Gandhi,*
> *Indian nationalist leader (1869-1948)*

EXAMPLE

Changing behaviour

Mary was incredibly intelligent and competent, with strong planning skills and a drive for results. The department achieved milestones every time they were set. However, morale was low and there was a blame culture; she was very efficient at spotting the flaw in an argument, and focused on this almost to the exclusion of everything else. The effect of this was that people were on the defensive, and ready to blame each other rather than support each other – and it was not an enjoyable place to be.

Through using these exercises, she learnt to trust people more and focus on what had gone well. The results are still there, but now, so are the employees!

PULLING it Together

Pulling it all together

Once all the preceding exercises are completed, review the results.

What are the messages? Use this data and your intuition (often not listened to enough!) to build a vision in your mind of what you will be like as a compelling, inspiring and motivating leader:

- What will you look like?

- What will the tone of your voice be, and what sort of language/phrases will you be using?

- How will you feel?

- What will your team see, hear and feel?

- What will your other stakeholders see, hear and feel?

- What one or a few words encapsulate this vision, so that whenever you want to bring this picture to mind you simply need to think or say these words?

KNOW Yourself

Assessing Personal Strengths and Blocks

As a leader, you may feel quite clear about the vision that you want to achieve. You may be less clear about your strengths and weaknesses – which are all too obvious to others. Doing a personal assessment can reveal hidden strengths as well as hidden problem areas. Here is a graphic tool to help you challenge yourself and give some time and thought to your current behaviour. If you have received 'interesting' feedback, this helps you attain deeper insight and perspective. The objective is to understand the reasons behind your current behaviours, so that you can make changes that are appropriate to you.

Going through these exercises, really spend time thinking and challenging yourself so you understand the reasons for the current behaviours that do not support your new vision. Truly understand what the benefits are to you of this behaviour and how you might get these benefits in a different way.

EXERCISE

Strengths / Blocks / Reasons why

1. Take a piece of paper and copy the picture below.
Leave plenty of space above and below the diagram.

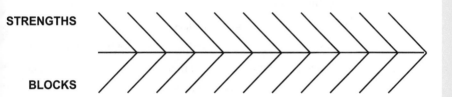

STRENGTHS

BLOCKS

2. Now brainstorm and list your current strengths
above the line. Think about what comes naturally
to you, and the feedback you've received in the
past from people who have appreciated your style.
Feel free to add more lines, or leave some blank.
Sometimes it is all too easy to focus on weaknesses,
but you will have very many strengths and not all
will be visible to you. So it is important to be fully
aware of these strengths both from your own
perspective and from the perspective of others
including bosses, peers and subordinates.

3. Next, underneath the line, brainstorm and list what's currently stopping you today. Record one "block" per line. Feel free to add more lines, or leave some blank as appropriate. Focus especially on behaviours you currently adopt that do not fit your vision.

These blocks may be internal to you or external, such as the working environment or company culture. It is also important to bear in mind that some blocks will be out of your direct control; you can control yourself and your behaviours, but you cannot control the behaviour of others nor the environment. So focus on what you can directly control.

4. Once you have identified all these blocks, ask of each one "What does that do for me?" "What does that give me?" Listen to your gut feel and trust what comes to mind. The reason for asking these questions is that even if it is a block it will be providing some benefit to you, otherwise you wouldn't be doing it. However, it is up to you to decide whether the block is worth keeping, and what you can do to change it if necessary.

"Always bear in mind that your own resolution to succeed is more important than any other one thing."
Abraham Lincoln

EXAMPLE

Learning to let go

Helen was a Senior Director in the the Marketing function of a global organisation. She was a very driven, results oriented and independent individual. Technically, she was very strong and well known for her technical abilities and amazing vision – and she had saved the company significant amounts of money. However, this clear line of sight and independence left a 'trail of bodies' across the organisation and within her team. The team felt disempowered and demotivated, and were not being developed personally or professionally.

These exercises helped Helen see that these very real strengths were also impeding the overall running of the function, as well as eroding her internal network – over time her position was becoming untenable. She was losing influence with her peer group as fewer and fewer people would work with her, despite the vision and technical strength she brought. She was working very long hours, which was causing pressure at home.

It was fascinating for her to understand the underlying reasons for her behaviours, (the "what it did for me") which was largely a fear of being out of control and of not being valued if she let go and allowed the team to "do the work".

By letting go and spending more time leading and developing the team, the overall department achieved much more and Helen re-built her influence with the senior management group of the Company enabling her to realise her vision. She also reduced her working hours and overall felt much happier and calmer in herself.

Dealing with Conflict

As soon as groups of people interact, there are differences of opinion and conflicts of interests. Although conflict is something most people want to avoid, handling conflict well could be the most important element for high performance and productivity.

Conflict can be both positive as well as negative in outcome, and is therefore not automatically something to be avoided. That being said, here are some tips that may reduce the likelihood of negative conflict.

Tips

- At the outset, for example of a project, take time to understand what the other person or people need and start from where you all agree. In particular, agree on the vision and big outcomes before you start the work. Understand where potential areas of disagreement may arise and then agree how to work these. When these areas of disagreement do arise, take time to brainstorm all the different options as openly and creatively as possible, so that each person achieves their goal without compromise. (Compromise means that no-one gets what they want.)

- Separate the individuals from the problem. Focus on the problem and maintain respect for the individuals at all times. This will help ensure a win-win approach, and therefore ongoing commitment. Avoid making defensive comments or judgemental remarks about others.

- Be as open minded as possible about what you want; the more you are, the more you are likely to achieve your goals from a range of options. Focus on the outcome, rather than becoming fixated in one position; often everyone is agreed on the overall outcome especially if all are employed within one organisation.

- Take a break and reflect, to ease the tension. This can be a useful way of giving people space and time to think and if necessary, calm down. This is a good influencing tool and is distinct from avoidance, as the individuals return to the topic, whether it's after a few minutes or a few days. This also often enables the individual to retain emotional control (a key strength in emotional intelligence and performance).

- Finally, conflict is often introduced when there is a lack of transparency amongst people, so focus on giving and receiving feedback. Getting feedback is a great way to open up communication. Before asking for feedback, especially with subordinates ask the following questions:

1. How do you think you did?

2. If you were to do it again, what would you do the same and how would you do it differently?

EXAMPLE

Regaining control

Billie was a leader in a manufacturing environment who used to get stressed from high volumes of work. Her release was to shout at others within the department (interestingly, not to those outside the department). This created a very difficult environment. Her colleagues felt they were constantly treading on eggshells and after a while they no longer wished to tolerate this behaviour.

Through coaching, Billie learned how to recognise when she felt she was losing control. She found that taking a break was an effective way to return to the discussion, feeling energised and constructive. This break needed only to be a walk of around 10 minutes and was very helpful at creating some emotional distance from the stress and regain a sense of perspective. Other tips she gained were:

- Arriving at work at least 15 minutes before the first meeting
- Remembering to plan in time to do the work rather than filling the whole day or week with meetings
- Learning to delegate more effectively and trusting others to do their jobs, by agreeing the work to be done and the date it would be done by and promising not to keep asking the status
- Accepting that she cannot control everything. There are some things we can control, some things we can influence, and some things we have absolutely no control over. There is no point in worrying about what you cannot control!

Managing TIME

Managing time is a key requirement in managing the demands of everyday life. People often complain of having too much to do and not enough time to do it and becoming stressed by this. This is completely understandable! However, if we accept that we have too much to do, and will not get everything done, this frees us to then determine what the priorities are.

Stress is often the result of feeling out of control, and at work can be through having too much work to do (quantitative) and/or too much work that we don't know how to do (qualitative).

Below are some tips that may help you improve your time management skills and attitudes.

Tips

- Focus on being clear about what is important to accomplish, whether it be on an annual basis, monthly, weekly or daily basis. Understanding this will then enable you to prioritise how your time is spent. Don't spend time on stuff that isn't necessary (unless it gives you a break for a few minutes). Stephen Covey's Time Management Matrix in his book, The Seven Habits of Highly Effective People, is a useful tool for sorting through and prioritising.

- Prioritise your tasks – be clear what has to be achieved today, or this week and then ruthlessly de-prioritise other pressures. Often prioritising on a weekly rather than daily basis keeps stress levels at bay as it's a longer time frame, so if you have one day that doesn't go according to plan you have some time to catch up.

- Know that sometimes you have to help others even if it doesn't help yourself. This is just part of life, but will also build your network/influencing power.

- Keep free time in your diary each week – don't fill it with back-to-back meetings. This will give you time to reflect, plan, and complete unexpected work. This could be some time each day, or one day per week, for example working from home – do whatever works best for you. Have you noticed the motorways are clearer on a Friday?!

- Email can be a huge help, but also a huge distractor. Turn the volume off so you don't hear every time you get an email. Review your in-box no more than 2-3 times per day, so you can concentrate on your priorities. Email can occupy significant amounts of time, but not always on what's important – it appears to be urgent because it's instantaneous, but it may not be.

- Take some time to plan for meetings. So much time can be wasted as individuals rush into a meeting straight from the last one, (and often late) and then it takes perhaps 10 minutes or more for everyone to be ready to concentrate and remember why they are there! It's not a criticism – we've all been there, but it's a scary thought to add this time up and multiply it by the number of attendees (and their salaries) to think of the cost implications. Think about the outcomes you want from the meeting – this is a key starting point to influence others. If you don't know what you want, you can't influence.

- Finally, and very importantly, take time for lunch each day. Invest this time in your health and well being. Eat a healthy meal, and sit down to eat it – not on the run. This time is essential for yourself, and to give you time to reflect and re-gain a sense of perspective. It will refresh you for the afternoon.

EXERCISE

Important v Urgent grid

Allocate your daily tasks into the appropriate quadrant of the grid, according to how urgent and/or important they are. (Note that the Importance scale goes from low to high, while the Urgency scale goes from high to low).

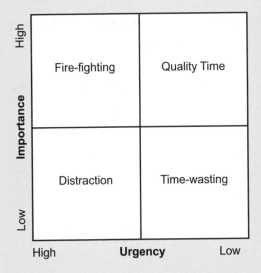

You should aim to maximise Quality Time dealing with Important tasks without the pressure of urgency, and the time spent Firefighting priorities will reduce. Improve your systems and processes for dealing with Distractions. Recognise Time-wasting tasks that might be 'nice to do' but not 'need to do' – perhaps save them up as 'rewards' if / when all the other tasks are completed.

SUMMARY

Creating the right leadership environment starts with yourself. Take time to create the vision of how you want to be that is true to who you are and is respectful of others.

Build a plan to accomplish this – know your natural strengths and develop these. Learn new skills to close any gaps.

Be aware of what blocks may impede the best of intentions, and calmly and confidently address them.

Stick to your resolutions – if you have a bad day, learn from it and start afresh.

Finally, enjoy the experience and the results of being a motivating leader of keen people. Won't it be great that others hold you up as a role model?!

"The key to successful leadership today is influence, not authority."
Kenneth Blanchard, US management author, presenter (b.1939)

Be the Apple of Everyone's Eye

EQ: The Vital Ingredient for Relationships that Work

by Tanya Yazdanpanahi

INTELLIGENT Emotions

A vital ingredient to creating great relationships at work

What's the need for Emotional Intelligence?

Most organisations prefer the work persona to be kept totally separate from anything more personal. So inappropriate outbursts, open displays of emotion, out of control behaviour, bullying, and 'throwing toys out of the pram' are quickly identified as emotional intelligence problems. Less obvious issues like having the wrong type of impact on colleagues, being closed down, bottled up, or unapproachable, present much subtler problems. All such behaviours demonstrate a need for raised EQ.

The Origins of EQ

Although recently popularised, the importance of emotional intelligence is by no means a new concept in life. Aspects of what has become known as "Emotional Intelligence" or (EQ) have been studied throughout the past few decades in areas such as child developmental psychology, health, marriage counselling, parenting and the business world to name just a few. The term "emotional intelligence" was created by Peter Salovey and Jack Mayer but it was Daniel Goleman who popularised the concepts for the world of work and leadership in his popular books *Emotional Intelligence* and *The New Leaders*. Goleman defines Emotional Intelligence as "the capacity for recognising our own feelings and those of others, for motivating ourselves, for managing emotions well in ourselves and in relationships". This capacity therefore includes areas such as self-awareness, awareness of others, adaptability, personal power, emotional expression, trustworthiness, assertiveness and empathy to name a just a few. So we can start to see what's behind this label 'Emotional Intelligence' and how we can go about heightening it.

It has been observed that the two recurring challenges most leaders have to tackle routinely in work situations are:

1. **Being able to truly engage with your stakeholders in order to achieve real success.**

2. **Being aware of your impact in the business when interacting with others.**

Both these challenges relate to how you interact with others and are, in fact, very inter-related. Interpersonal relationships and empathy are fundamental aspects of a person's emotional intelligence. These challenges have a huge impact on team dynamics, effective leadership, achievement of results and career progression. Many individuals facing these challenges have very high IQs (IQ is a measure of an individual's intellectual, analytical, logical and rational abilities). They are quick thinking, dynamic individuals. Yet their inability to recognise, understand and overcome these challenges, stops them from influencing with ease, managing their staff, and creating high traction in their organisations. Their ability to become truly successful and reach their real potential is compromised.

EQ is now also being measured quite effectively using diagnostics such as the 'ei' (from JCA (occupational psychologists) Ltd) and 'EQ-i' (The EQ Edge by Stein and Book). Understanding where you think you are against the various scales and where others may see you (360 version) is a good starting point in the journey to raising your EQ.

What few people know is that skills of Emotional Intelligence can be learned. Unlike IQ, which remains more or less static, EQ can be developed. Unlike IQ which is considered to be hard wired from birth, EQ can and does increase with age. The part of our brains which is responsible for regulating emotions is called the amygdala and the part responsible for our rational logical thought is called the neocortex. Interestingly, the emotional part of our brain was developed long before the neocortex as humans evolved!

In some situations people completely freeze in terror or lash out in an outburst of emotions. This has been termed by Goleman as the "amygdala hijack" and it is where the amygdala "hijacks" the brain and causes it to flood the body with stress hormones

related to our instinctive flight or fight responses. It does this so quickly and before the neocortex (prefrontal lobes) can mediate the reaction. The characteristics of the amygdala hijack is that the emotion is very strong, it is very sudden and often we regret our reaction and wish we had reacted differently.

The IMPORTANCE of EQ for Leaders

While the vast field of emotional Intelligence has much to
offer, there are two key areas that are worth particular focus.
According to an article by C & Leslie Chappelow in Leadership
in Action which was focussing on how to keep top executives
careers on track, the top two de-railers for leadership success
are:

- The inability to adapt and develop during
  periods of change

- The inability to establish strong interpersonal
  relationships

The ability to adapt and develop during periods of change is a
key aspect of **self management**. The ability to establish strong
interpersonal relationships produces effective **relationship
management**. Both of these are present in a person
with high emotional intelligence. What differentiates good
managers and great leaders from the ordinary, is how well they
demonstrate emotional intelligence skills. Today the trend of
most organisations is to pay more attention to these 'soft skills',
particularly in management roles, because it has proven to be
more effective.

Anyone can become angry – that is easy.
But to be angry with the right person, to the right degree, at the right time,
for the right purpose, and in the right way – this is not easy.
Aristotle, 384BC, The Nicomachean Ethics

APPROPRIATE Emotions

What makes emotions inappropriate? All human beings feel emotions. But you have a **choice** about how you respond to your emotions and also how you express them. Increasing your self awareness and understanding the link between your thoughts, your feelings and your actions, is core to your emotional intelligence. Essentially it is about learning to manage your emotional life with intelligence. There are many tools and techniques to help you to do this....

EXAMPLE

A Problem Engaging with Stakeholders

Andrew, a senior manager, excelled at being technically brilliant. He was extremely logical, analytical, quick thinking and very goal driven. Despite his amazing ability to solve the major logistical problems the business faced, his manager knew he needed coaching. He was 'leaving carnage in his wake' with regards to the people he interacted with. He showed almost no control over how he expressed his feelings: he was either ecstatic when something went right, or incredibly attacking and aggressive in meetings whenever he didn't get his way. He also had a tendency to "throw his teddy into a corner" when he didn't get what he wanted. Interestingly, this behaviour was seen only 10% of the time, but the noise it created was disproportionate. In short, he was getting a reputation.

Andrew definitely had some aspects of high emotional intelligence: self management. He was very goal driven, emotionally resilient and had a high sense of personal power. Andrew's problem was relationship management, particularly in certain situations. Given his high profile job, these key occasions were beginning to be 'known' around the business.

BEING Responsible for your Emotion

Managers who show such characteristics of low emotional intelligence need to learn how to take responsibility for their emotions. It is common to believe that emotions are caused by other people. For example, "You make me so angry when you are always late with a piece of work" or "I get so frustrated with the way that you never articulate what you need from me". It is true that the late work or the lack of articulation acts as a **stimulus** but that does not in fact **cause** the emotion in you. Something else does that. It is **your** need for **something** which we'll call x. Whatever x may be! Here is a great exercise to help people understand and take responsibility for their emotions.

EXERCISE

Taking Personal Responsibility for your Emotions

1. Whenever a person feels an emotion (positive or negative), ask them to identify that emotion. (IDENTIFY EMOTION)

2. Then ask them to think about the need or requirement that is either being met or not being met (by someone else or something else) which is causing that emotion? (THE NEED). Note: this may be difficult for them to recognise so this step may take some time.

3. Having understood that the emotion has been triggered by something they need or require and having identified that need, they can now give themselves some advice as to how they can meet that need in the future. (Note: This may not be necessary if the expressing of the emotion is not inappropriate)

This process helps an individual understand what is behind his or her emotions and thus increases self awareness. It also starts to embed the concept that you do have the ability to think about your emotions before you express them.

"Every minute you are angry,
you lose sixty seconds of happiness."
Ralph Waldo Emerson

Understanding what is behind emotions and increasing self awareness helps, but often it is not enough. People can intellectually appreciate that it is important to express emotions appropriately, but in practice old needs might re-surface. Sometimes there is a belief that 'you are right and therefore you should get your way!' Sadly, success in business does not come from simply 'being right'. What is often needed is to develop a different strategy to satisfy those trigger points when the need doesn't get met.

EQ Foundation Stones

The Dalai Lama may not call it emotional intelligence, but the timeless wisdom he clearly sets out in his instructions for life, perfectly describes the most essential and relevant qualities of EQ. His easy-to-remember three R's are:

- **Respect for self**
- **Respect for others**
- **Responsibility for all your actions**

The foundation stones of high emotional intelligence are: self regard (seeing your strengths and weaknesses in a positive frame), regard for others, self awareness and awareness of others. Although there are many other aspects such as trust, free expression, and interdependence, however these tend to manifest from the key foundation stones. Many have categorised all these aspects under two main headings: self management and relationship management.

Self Management

Self management includes our ability to be goal driven, have a sense of personal power and emotional resilience. It is about being in charge of ourselves. This is often referred to as intrapersonal intelligence.

Relationship Management

Relationship management includes our ability to form trusting relationships, be interdependent with others and be able to freely express our emotions to others in an appropriate way and have empathy and influence. This is often referred to as interpersonal intelligence.

REGARD for Self and Others

Regard for Yourself and Regard for Others

So what does 'regard for self' mean? This is about how much you really value yourself and accept yourself for who you are. That you see your strengths and your weaknesses in a positive light. Regard for others is about how much you really value and accept others for who they are regardless of whether you necessarily like them as friends or approve of their value system. Regard for others is about having regard for the people the way they are.

Healthy emotionally intelligent relationships are borne out of someone with high self regard and high regard for others. When either of these are low, aggressive, arrogant or bullying behaviour can manifest on the one hand and victim-like behaviour can manifest on the other. When both are low, hopeless situations arise where individuals neither value themselves (self regard) or the views, opinions or support of others (regard for others). This can often lead down a desperate road of mental and physical self destruction. Having high EQ is not only important in your working life, it can also be critical to your personal well being and health!

"He who smiles rather than rages is always the stronger."
Japanese wisdom

AWARENESS of Self and Others

Self Awareness and Awareness of Others

Self awareness means being aware of how you are feeling
physically, mentally and emotionally. Although this may seem
an obvious and natural quality, some people completely
cut themselves off from their own feelings and sensations.
Awareness of others refers to how aware you are of what's
going on for others around you: how are they feeling physically,
mentally and emotionally. People with high emotional
intelligence successfully 'read' other people's body language
and correctly interpret changes in that person's state. But some
people completely lack awareness about how other people
might be feeling. They simply don't notice.

CHECKING the Foundations...

Self Regard and Regard for Others

How you feel about yourself and how you are feeling about others, very much determines the types of relationships you develop. How can you begin to increase your level of EQ? First, through simple exploration and reflection, you need to assess whether you have high or low self regard and high or low regard for others. Having high self regard and high regard for others is fundamental for high EQ and healthy relationships. This is the goal! However, there may be times when you don't find yourself in this ideal place. So through exploring and understanding the patterns that you may be experiencing in different situations with different people, you can begin to understand what to do to increase both of these fundamental aspects of EQ.

EXAMPLE

Flamboyant Emotions

Whenever Emma felt an emotion she expressed it immediately - with very little thought in between. Sometimes it was anger or frustration and sometimes it might be anxiety or sadness. Other times it could be joy and excitement! Emma's variable emotions made quite a negative impact. The senior stakeholders were loosing confidence in her - especially when she expressed negative emotions in very inappropriate situations. She was seen to lack self confidence some of the time and appeared arrogant at other times.

The key to raising her self awareness came through a thorough exploration of the 'OK Corral*'. She began to understand the situations, types of people and times when she visited the 'I'm OK, You're OK, I'm Not OK, You're Not OK' Quadrants. Emma spent much of her time being in the boxes that she labelled "Victim" (I'm not OK / You're OK) and "frustrated" (I'm OK/You're not OK). She never associated into the box labelled 'Bully'. She moved from 'Victim' to 'Frustrated' and back to 'Victim'.

Then she explored what was in her Healthy box (I'm OK/ You're OK) when she had healthy and emotionally intelligent relationships. These only happened outside of work with her close family. By recognising this positive pattern, Emma was able to stand back and think about how (if she found herself in Victim or Frustrated quadrants) she could move into the Healthy space.

The 'OK Corral' is a very simple and effective technique for exploration, drawing on the theories of Transactional Analysis. In the model on the next page, "I'm OK" refers to high self regard and conversely, "I'm not OK" refers to low self regard. Similarly, "You're OK" refers to high regard for others and "You're not OK" refers to low regard for others. Each quadrant represents a different type of relationship. Sometimes you can often find yourself in all four quadrants in the same conversation! However, what is more usual is that you find yourself in specific quadrants, i.e. there is a pattern of how you behave with specific people and specific situations.

This exercise can help you recognise the patterns that may exist. It also identifies when you find yourself in the "healthy" relationships. This is important to help you to be at your best most of the time.

EXERCISE

OK Corral

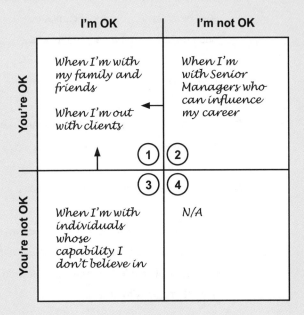

	I'm OK	**I'm not OK**
You're OK	When I'm with my family and friends / When I'm out with clients	When I'm with Senior Managers who can influence my career
You're not OK	When I'm with individuals whose capability I don't believe in	N/A

1. Define what high self regard and low self regard looks, feels and sounds like for you?

2. Define what high regard for others and low regard for others looks, feels and sounds like for you?

3. Start to think about when you are in each of the quadrant – write these down in the relevant quadrants.

4. What are the circumstances that exist that are likely to get you into each of those quadrants?

(These may be internal or inner things such as your beliefs and values, or your attitudes. It could also be external or outer circumstances, such as having to present to the senior management team or conducting performance appraisals)

5. What do you say and do when you are in each of these areas?

6. How do you feel when you are in each?

7. For the three quadrants 2, 3, 4, do you ever get out of these quadrants and move towards a healthy relationship (quadrant 1)? How do you do this? (Indicate with arrows)

8. For the Healthy quadrant, what characterises being in this place with other people? What can you learn from this?

9. What would you like to change? What pattern would you like to have at work?

Despite this being a simple model, the words and patterns that emerge can give great insights and potential momentum for change.

CONTINUING to Build Self Awareness

The second area to focus on at this initial discovery stage is checking where you are around your own self awareness. In fact, simply reflecting in any way about how you are behaving in certain environments, how you are feeling, and what you are thinking will have the effect of raising your self awareness 'bank account'! The following exercise is another way of doing this.

How often do you check in with how you are feeling? Unless it is a really strong emotion like a positive feeling of extreme joy or a negative feeling of anger or sadness, you may discover you are less aware of subtle feelings.

Emotional Check Ins

Quite commonly, people lack a good, accurate vocabulary to describe their feelings because knowing how to identify or think about these emotions has not been developed. The connection between the logical, rational, thinking part of the brain, and the part that is responsible for emotions, needs to get stronger. Keeping an "emotional diary" is one way to start to strengthen that link. Simply keep tabs on your feelings throughout the day – write them down.

EXERCISE

Tracking your emotional path

Copy the template from the example below, and record the emotions you are feeling throughout the day. As you plot the path, write in the context of what is happening, about to happen or maybe has happened. Try this for a week!

This exercise not only prompts you to record how you are feeling at different points in the day but also helps you to measure the intensity (positive and negative) throughout the day and plot what may be triggering them. Think carefully about how to describe the emotion, even if it isn't extreme. Avoid just using words like "fine" and 'good'. Stretch yourself to go beyond the evaluation and identify what kind of emotion you are feeling. Reflecting on your week's emotional diary will reveal patterns that may be emerging that you were not previously aware of. Although it may seem difficult at the start, this process gets progressively easier with practice.

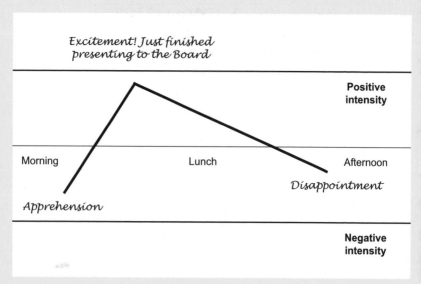

READING Emotions

Reading the Expression of Emotions

Your emotions and how they are perceived by others are important. When there's an absence of expression, people often assume the negative. People sense you as being emotionally "closed" or holding back on expressing emotions. They assume you wouldn't hold back positive emotions, so you must be bottling up something negative.

EXAMPLE

The Wrong Sort of Impact

Even though quite young, Ellen showed such high potential, she was being fast tracked in the organisation. For the first 5 years of her career, she had been mainly an individual contributor. Now she was starting to work on cross functional teams before being given a management position. Although she was very bright, she obviously had problems interacting with people at work. The feedback given was that people couldn't read her emotions. Her facial expressions were almost always blank, so people tended to read her as negative. They assumed she wasn't happy with them or something they had said or done. Not surprisingly, they found it uncomfortable working with her. Given the fact she needed to influence people that didn't directly work with her and that she didn't interact with on a regular basis, this mis-read of her body language was causing significant problems. This could potentially have held her career back. Ellen was totally unaware of this issue until feedback from her manager brought to her attention.

Learning how to keep an Emotional Diary was difficult for Ellen, but she succeeded, and gradually learned to find the right vocabulary to describe her feelings and feel comfortable showing her emotions to others.

CONTROLLED Emotions

Over-controlled and Under-controlled emotions

Many people think that emotions have no place at work, so they strive to maintain a blank screen. They erroneously believe that this will be perceived as more business like. However, when an individual is unable to freely express themselves (appropriately) it can result in low EQ. When emotions get bottled up or buried, this is over-control. The danger is that such over-control may result in highly charged and inappropriate emotional outbursts on the one hand, or even long-term illness on the other.

This can be thought of in terms of a balloon that is getting pumped up and up and up. There comes a point that unless some of the air is released, the balloon will burst! Being free and in charge of your emotions is about releasing that air when you need to and maybe not releasing it at other times, as well as deciding how you want to release it. The ideal is to be in control of your emotions and know how big you want your balloon to be. When individuals have under-control of their emotions, they have no thought process linked to their feelings or emotions. They feel them and release them regardless of anything or anyone – this, again results in very low EQ! It's like having a totally deflated balloon all of the time.

EXERCISE

Developing a New Strategy for Emotional Expression

1. Visualise and talk through (with someone else or to yourself out loud) the situation which caused the inappropriate expression of an emotion.

2. Think about what you were thinking about just prior to expressing the emotion (Trigger point). This trigger will have been caused by your need or requirement either being met or not being met. When your needs are met, you will feel/express positive emotions. When your needs don't get met, you will feel/express a negative emotion.

3. Step out of your "shoes" and imagine you could step into the position of an "observer" who is watching the scenario described in step 1 above.

4. Play this scenario again as though it was a film on a screen.

5. Now imagine you are an objective observer and give yourself the best advice about what new strategy to take, whenever you get triggered. This new strategy must meet your need or requirement in the end.

6. Rewind and watch this new film showing the new strategy you have advised yourself on. Check it out to make sure it works!

7. Commit to practicing this new strategy as soon as possible and enjoy the improved effect.

TRUST

Why is it easy to express your emotions with some people and not with others? When people have difficulty expressing their emotions, sometimes it indicates a trust issue. Having the ability to be carefully trusting of others and know your criteria for trusting someone is another important indicator of high EQ. What are your criteria for trust? Do you find it easy to trust people or do you mistrust them most of the time? What is your natural inclination when you meet new people? Who you feel comfortable expressing emotions with, and who you do not, depends on your level of trust. This, in turn, is intertwined with the level of perceived risk you feel. Through re-evaluating your criteria, it is possible to learn how to default to a more carefully trusting attitude – more quickly – rather than always being mistrustful, or, indeed, over-trusting.

EXERCISE

Circles of Trust

Aim: To identify who sits in which circle and why?

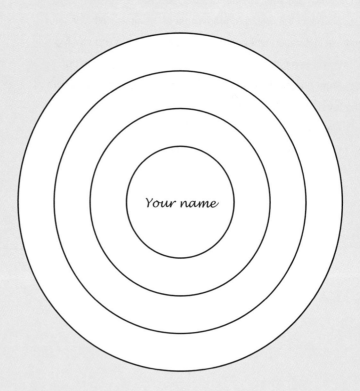

1. Without any real criteria for what each circle represents place different people in your life (personal and work) into the relevant circles. (Do not give any definitions of the various circles to ensure that the criteria are not being pre-defined)

2. Why have you placed each person where you have? (This question will extract their definitions)

3. What is it about how you feel towards the people in that circle that are similar?

4. What are the differences between the different circles?

5. How can someone move from one circle to another (in either direction)?

Answering these questions carefully will raise your self awareness and increase your EQ.

AWARENESS of others

Many people fear that paying attention to how other people may be feeling may seem rude, intrusive, or disrespectful. How could it be possible to know what another person is feeling? This isn't about mind reading, it is about raising your awareness of others, just noticing. How do you think they are feeling physically? What do you think they are thinking about? What's their frame of mind today? What emotions do you think they are feeling at any given point? Can you tell? How? Once you start to observe more carefully how people look, what they do, say, and the actual language they use, you may start to realise how easy and obvious the signs are. How could you have missed these signals before? Knowing this is invaluable when thinking about how you relate to them.

EXAMPLE

Blind spots

Craig was a highly personable and gregarious man. He was popular, bright and highly ambitious. When he was presenting however, he failed to take his audience with him. He was completely unaware of the negative impact he was making. Because he was very intelligent and understood his discipline so well, he expected everyone to think the same way he did. He assumed his peers were in full agreement. He also believed that because he was extremely successful, he could expect an imminent promotion. Unfortunately, how others perceived him was totally different! The only thing that could break through this super positive self belief would be a very precisely designed 360-degree feedback with specifically tailored questions. 360-degree feedback works best when a third party pulls it together and draws out themes. Through exploring his feedback, Craig finally realised the effect he was having. Luckily, he was smart enough to make the necessary changes.

Getting Craig to see things through others' eyes was a key next step after the 360 degree feedback. That achieved greater self-awareness. Greater awareness of others was achieved using the following exercise. It is simple exercise but so effective and uses the same technique (of taking different perceptual positions) as the exercise on "Developing a New Strategy" that was outlined earlier in the chapter and has been used in previous chapters. Over time, your awareness of others is truly heightened and because this is a quick tool it can be easily used in the moment.

EXERCISE

360 Feedback Questions to Increase Self Awareness

1. How does [person x] contribute to the business?
2. How does his/her style enhance this contribution?
3. How does his/her style hinder this contribution?
4. What should they stop doing or do less of?
5. What should they start doing or do more of?
6. If you could change one aspect of the way [person x] interacts with you and others, what would that be?
7. What would this achieve for them, in your opinion?
8. What would be the most helpful piece of advice that you could give [person x] on the way that they "interact with others"?

It is important that the person begins to see things through other people's eyes and understands the similarities and differences between their perspective and others. Many people operate from a position that everyone thinks like they do – or they should! The brighter they are and the more they know, the more they expect everyone else to think the same way.

When conducting a feedback exercise, it's so important to contract with the person receiving feedback at the start of the process. Getting buy-in to the questions or even shaping the questions together at the start is vital. Establishing the ground rules such as how the feedback will be collected, levels of disclosure and honesty ensure that meaningful discussions can be had.

EXERCISE

Standing in your Audiences' Shoes

1. Identify and describe a specific situation where you were working less well with an individual?

2. Now step out of your skin and climb into their skin (physically move to their position). Take a moment to really feel, think and behave as they would. Imitate any mannerisms that they may have! Understand what makes them tick.

3. Now, still in their skin, look at yourself through their eyes and describe (in their words) what they are seeing, thinking, feeling and hearing?

4. Now step out of their skin and move to the corner of the room and look towards where you and the other person were sitting. You are no longer you or the other person, but an external coach who has come to help you.

5. Run the scenario again as if it was a film

6. Now give (name yourself) 3 pieces of advice about how you could think and behave differently given your newly acquired awareness of the other person's position?

7. Repeat steps 1- 6 using a specific situation where you were working well with an individual?

8. What is the similarity and differences between these bits of advice that you have given yourself?

EMOTIONS: A Dirty Word?

To be successful in business we have to build effective relationships with each other – it's the oil in the organisation and between organisations. Developing emotional intelligence has been shown to be profound in its effects in the workplace and therefore the juice is most definitely worth the squeeze. To be able to engage productively with your stakeholders and maintain effective relationships, to be able to influence and motivate others as well as yourself, to have empathy, rapport and be expressive – are all EQ skills that can be developed. However, because raising EQ is about changing some fundamental inner programming, practice, practice and more practice will be the only way to sustain change longer term.

You do have choice about how you respond to your emotions. You certainly have choice over how you express them and when. The insights and effective techniques presented in this chapter are just a few of the many tools you can use to raise your EQ. Imagine being able to cope through all kinds of change. You can learn how to have regard for yourself, for others, awareness of yourself and others. You can be totally responsible for your feelings and actions. Emotions don't have to be a dirty word at work anymore.

The Fruit Salad of Life

of Life

How to Juggle your
Work:Life Balance

by Liz Hunt

WORKING out your Life Balance

You only live once. You only have one life in which to explore and find out what makes your heart sing. You only have one life to achieve the things that will truly satisfy you. Therefore, crafting this life is crucial to creating what you've always dreamed of, and crucial to your happiness. Mastering the art of balancing your life forms the vital basis of your decisions, choices and negotiations. This delicate balance not only needs to incorporate other people's plans, but also requires regular updates. Just as your life changes and evolves over time, so do your feelings, needs and boundaries. Reviewing what is important to you will keep you in the black. You can't afford the cost of neglecting early warning signals. Be forewarned and ready to rectify situations that could put you and your health at risk.

What is meant by work/life balance?

Lots of people talk about wanting a better work/life balance. Most people know when their life is out of balance. There's pressure to achieve work targets, challenging deadlines and increased travel. 'Time' has become the most desirable 'must-have' product. Everyone wants more. For some, having more time means feeling 'more in control'; or having more time with family and friends; or being able to meet those goals, targets and deadlines at work; or wanting to achieve more in our lives; or just simply having time to relax.

"When shall we live if not now?"
Seneca, Roman Philosopher & Dramatist, 65 A.D

Does that mean an equal balance between work & life?

When your life is out of balance, it is often tempting to imagine working much less and having masses of leisure time. But in reality, planning an equal number of hours for business and personal activities is probably unrealistic. Perhaps a more energising way to establish better balance is to carefully assess what works for you right now. You are probably already aware of how different your needs were years ago. What works when you are single, what works when you are married, what works when you have children, when you start a new career or when you near retirement - all of these phases of life will require different mixtures of work/life balance. How can you tune in and determine the best balance for any phase of life? Is there a perfect formula to strive for?

"Don't sweat the small stuff ... and it's all small stuff."
Richard Carlson

EXAMPLE

When the lights don't twinkle – the balance is wrong!
A Senior Manager working in the pharmaceutical industry had a very highly paid and responsible position with lots of international travel. Unfortunately, just as the demands of his organisation increased, his immediate manager left and was not replaced. He took up the slack for a while, but the strain proved intolerable. After several months of overwork, he had a breakdown.

Now he works for a new company and earns less money. With a lower salary, he and his family moved out of London. But the positive perk was getting to spend more time with his boys. He got involved in helping out with the Cubs, and became Cub Leader. He delights in designing the session each week. One of his best experiences was teaching the boys to wire up a small bulb to a battery and teaching them the basics of Morse Code. As they turned off the lights in the village hall, all they could see were the twinkling lights as the boys sent messages to each other. His Monday night class teaching these boys taught him the real value of work/life balance. Now, if work ever starts to encroach on these Monday nights, he just has to remind himself of those little twinkling lights that inspire him and he readjusts his priorities.

EXERCISE

Assess whether you have an effective Work/Life Balance

Because each phase of life requires a different balance, it is a good idea to review and re-assess how well you are doing. Here are some questions to assist you in spotting some early warning signals.

1. Do you enjoy less than 60% of your work and has it been like this for some time? ....Yes ☐ No ☐

2. Do you feel you don't have the time to do all the things you want to do? ....Yes ☐ No ☐

3. Do you feel that what you've got is not what you want any more? ....Yes ☐ No ☐

4. Have you forgotten what's important to you? ....Yes ☐ No ☐

5. Do you lack the energy to do the things that you want to do? ....Yes ☐ No ☐

6. Have things been unclear and ambiguous for too long? ....Yes ☐ No ☐

7. Do you feel you are not getting enough satisfaction in your life? ....Yes ☐ No ☐

8. Do you feel that your needs are at the bottom of the pile? Are your needs getting squashed or disregarded? ....Yes ☐ No ☐

9. Have you noticed that things that used to satisfy you are not satisfying you now? ....Yes ☐ No ☐

10. Do you find yourself caught between conflicting objectives? ....Yes ☐ No ☐

11. Do you feel that you are not in control or are out of control? ....Yes ☐ No ☐

12. Are you worried that your hours at work have increased significantly over time and you do not see an end to it? ....Yes ☐ No ☐

13. Are you having trouble sleeping or waking feeling unrefreshed for no apparent reason? ....Yes ☐ No ☐

14. Have you noticed that you have less energy or enthusiasm for sorting out problems? ....Yes ☐ No ☐

15. Are you sensing that your productivity is decreasing? Do you feel you are working a lot of hours but are not getting anywhere or feeling satisfied? ....Yes ☐ No ☐

16. Have things changed around you but you have not fundamentally changed? ....Yes ☐ No ☐

17. Are you feeling stressed by what you do or how you think? ....Yes ☐ No ☐

18. Are you are feeling more insecure or losing confidence? ....Yes ☐ No ☐

19. Are you are regularly missing out or cancelling your own activities that you enjoy? ....Yes ☐ No ☐

20. Have you lost your sense of

humour or fun? ....Yes ☐ No ☐

Scoring

Add up the number of questions with a 'YES' answer.

If you scored 1-3:

There may be a few areas you need to review.

If you scored 3-10:

Some areas of your life need reflection: Do these answers reflect your reality? Take some time out to use the tools in this chapter. See what you need to renegotiate so that you can enjoy your life more.

If you scored 10-20:

It's time to take a serious look at your life and what you want from it. It could be that each area of your life is manageable on its own, but not when they are added together. This may not be fulfilling or satisfying you. If your energy is being drained, over time, this may damage your health. Sometimes even the thought of taking time out seems overwhelming. When you don't know where to start, external support from a friend or coach can help.

3 Reasons

Three reasons why you can't afford to neglect this balance

If you've ever been tempted to think that your life will take care of itself, or that you don't have choice over improving the balance because your job requires you to be present five days a week, think again. There are three important reasons why you must pay attention to work/life balance:

1. The impact on emotional and physical health

When you are not enjoying your life over a long period of time, this stress will impact on your psychological and physical health. When you are out of kilter, this puts a strain on all your relationships. Working with business colleagues becomes beset with misunderstandings, frustration and things not going smoothly. Family relationships suffer from increased tension. Your personal relationships or marriage will also be badly affected. Being around someone whose life balance is out of kilter can be chaotic, stressful, tense, depressing, ambiguous, frustrating, infuriating. Everyone feels resentful, unhappy, irritated, angry, sad ... basically - it's not fun!

2. Decreased productivity

Working too long or too hard over sustained periods of time decreases energy and creates fatigue. For the economy in the UK, poor work/life balance leads to a decrease in productivity and an increase of wasted time due to the impaired ability to create clear goals, set boundaries and access the energy needed to **stay focused** in a world of competing requests.

3. Chaotic Objectives

When the work/life balance is off-kilter, planning ability suffers.

Often this leads to frequent changes of direction, or just not being clear about direction. Sometimes, in a effort to mask the chaos, people pull rank in an attempt to instil some order. All of this contributes to a feeling of being out of control. How can objectives be met if the goals are unclear or constantly changing?

"One of the symptoms of nervous breakdown is the belief that one's work is terribly important."
Bertrand Russell

The **HAMSTER WHEEL** of Life

Here are some of the most common questions people express about work/life balance. Do you ever hear yourself say the following:

- It doesn't do it for me any more
- I feel I'm not satisfied
- There's something missing.
- Things that used to satisfy me are not satisfying me anymore
- It feels like I'm treading water
- I don't have time to do all the things I want to do
- I'm not sure what's important to me anymore
- I'm not enjoying myself

Statements like these generally indicate that a person needs to review some aspect of their life. Then they might realise that perhaps they have been doing things for someone else, or for some reason that is no longer important to them or it never was. Or it could be that what pleased them in the past no longer fits their new phase of life. They've been there, done that, and got the T-shirt! It's time to move on. Often this habitual behaviour crept up on them. They willingly gave in to the demands of others and their time got filled up for months or years. If this has happened, it might be crucial to re-evaluate what is important, which obligations need to be fulfilled and what is possible to change.

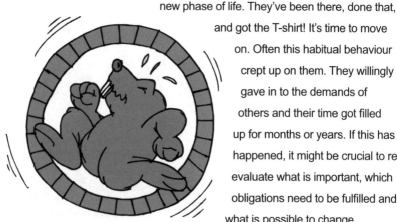

EXERCISE

Wheel of Life

To see what's going on in your life complete the following exercise.

1. Draw a pie chart to illustrate the various areas of your life and their importance to you.

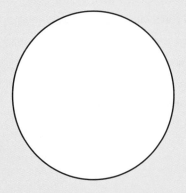

2. Now draw another one with the % of time you actually spend doing each activity.

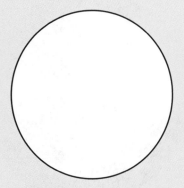

What does this tell you? How do you feel about this? What's OK? What do you want to spend less time doing? What is the gap? What's something you'd like to change?

41% of your Life is spent at Work!

It is estimated that you spend at least 41% of your life at work. On average, you spend 30% of your life asleep and another 15% travelling, shopping, bathing etc. There's not much chance for anything else. So work is unavoidably a part of life. But is 'life' actually a separate alternative to work? If work never feels enjoyable, but always leads to boredom, irritation, frustration, bitterness, confusion and guilt, then 41% of your life will feel miserable! If you'd rather not be at work at all, such attitudes do not encourage optimum performance. How differently would you feel if you found ways to enjoy doing all your tasks, delivered excellent service, managed your resources well, and came up with ideas better than the competitors?

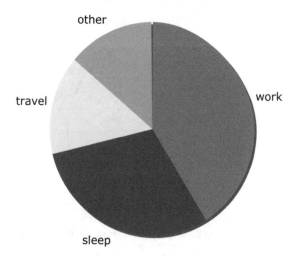

EXAMPLE

"But Darling, I'm doing it for the family"

A Regional Sales Director for a large national company spent many hours on the road travelling from one area to another, motivating his sales team and striving to meet deadlines and targets. He spent days away from home each week tending his patch. When his then wife complained, questioned or challenged that he was away too much, he said to her, "But Darling, I'm doing this for the family!" This pacified her for a while... until the next time.

After years of behaving this way, his marriage broke down and they split up. A year later, he became disenchanted with his job and resigned with a view to considering his career options. While rethinking his life, he realised he wasn't doing 'all those hours for the family'. He realised he was doing all those hours for himself. He said, "I loved being in the cut and thrust of the business. I loved zooming from one area of the country to another. I loved the dinners with clients and staying in hotels. I realised that it was all about me. But I also realised what a mistake it was to lose the woman I loved, who is the mother of my children. I realised my sons didn't know who their father was and didn't have a male role model of how to relate to men. I just couldn't see it before and probably couldn't have been honest about it then."

What he used to believe was not really the truth. His insistence that he was 'doing it for the family' gave his wife no room to argue. Sadly, the subsequent loss of work/life balance cost him dearly.

With coaching, he recognised that his drive and love for the fast lane fuelled his passion. So, in his new relationship, he chose to explain his needs so they could both understand and manage his dynamic energy better. When he takes it too far, she just smiles, realising it's what makes him who he is, and gently tells him the impact it's having on them!

The Work:Life SOLUTION

Achievement and Enjoyment

Have you ever envied people who say that their work is fun? Oddly enough, you can find them in almost every profession. Somehow their ability to achieve seems to be tied inextricably to their ability to enjoy what they do. Because they are having so much fun, they enjoy the process of whatever they are doing, thinking and planning, and their performance soars. Their enjoyment does not depend only on completing the task.

Two Key Factors of Effective Work/Life Balance

Economic conditions and social demands have changed the nature of work. Work used to be a matter of necessity and survival. Although work is still a necessity today, more focus is now based on two simple values:

- Daily achievement
- Enjoyment

Although this may seem so simplistic as to be irrelevant, don't underestimate the deeper values that these satisfy. Achievement and Enjoyment answer the big question 'Why?'. Why do you want a better income?...a new house?...the kids through college?...to do a good job today?...to come to work at all? What you feel you've achieved, what you can measure and develop, satisfies a deeper value of growth and contribution. When your role doesn't give you that sense of achievement, you'll find it hard to feel satisfied. If you can't see that your work has created a tangible product you can feel proud of, or that you have contributed in some way, you won't feel fulfilled.

"More men are killed by overwork than the importance of the work justifies."
(Joseph) Rudyard Kipling

Enjoyment means more than just having a good time, it means pride, satisfaction, happiness, celebration, fun, love, and a sense of wellbeing....all the joys of living. People who enjoy doing a good job at whatever they do, who take pride in their work, who spend quality moments assisting others and celebrating wins, usually feel much more happy and fulfilled .

The 'As Soon As' Trap

Focusing on Achievement and Enjoyment every day not only helps you get the full value from life, it is the perfect antidote to the 'As Soon As' trap. When people dream about doing what they really want to do 'as soon as' something else happens, this saps their energy. It's as if they live their lives on 'hold', waiting for that perfect day when they finally get to fulfil their dreams and enjoy themselves. Have you ever caught yourself thinking you will be able to do something important:

> ... as soon as the kids are at school
> ... as soon as I've paid off my mortgage
> ... as soon as the kids go to university
> ... as soon as we've done this house up
> ... as soon as ... (fill in your own blanks)

"When I hear somebody sigh 'Life is hard',
I am always tempted to ask, 'compared to what?'"
Sydney Harris

EXERCISE

Measure Your Levels of Enjoyment & Achievement

Measuring your 'Achievement' means looking at the small wins as much as the big wins. Things like finishing an onerous task on time, helping someone else learn something, saying just the right thing at the right time, or changing a habit. Measuring 'Enjoyment' doesn't just mean when you have time off to have a good time or socialise. It also means acknowledging every little moment when you've felt proud, satisfied, happy, supportive or appreciated.

Fill in the Quadrant below as you ask yourself the following questions.

- When was the last time you Achieved AND Enjoyed something at work?
- What have you Achieved AND Enjoyed with your family?
- When have you Achieved AND Enjoyed with your friends?
- How recently have you Achieved AND Enjoyed something just for you?

Work	**Family**
Friends	**Self**

The places where you have both achievement and enjoyment boost your energy and make your life more enjoyable. Notice when these occur and ask yourself:

- How can I ensure that I do more of these things in my life?"

- Who else can help me create more achievement and enjoyment?

Why not take 20 minutes on the way home from work and do something just for yourself? Watch a sunset. Talk a walk. Have a coffee and read the paper. And as you turn the key in the door, think about what you want to focus on this evening when you enter the house. Commit to whatever will give you that sense of achieving or enjoying, or both...then act accordingly when you do walk in the door.

EXAMPLE

Inner Conflict

A Manager confessed that although he often espoused that
his family was the most important thing for him, he realised
that he spent far more time at work. He felt guilty about this,
especially because he had promised his wife that he would
reduce his work hours. In fact, this never happened, because
at a subconscious level, he had a conflict. What his work gave
him was a very important sense of achievement, plus lots
of enjoyment. But his family were very important to him too,
because he also had high levels of achievement and enjoyment
at home. So he worked out which bits of his work gave him
the most sense of achievement. By devoting more of his time
to these, he was able to free up more time to spend with his
family.

"In the middle of difficulty lies opportunity."
Albert Einstein

YOUR Personal Brand

Companies invest a great deal of money and research into getting the 'Brand' right. They know that people buy brands because they want to be associated with what a particular brand signifies. The brand they choose gives a message about what culture they belong to. The brand makes a statement about who they are, how successful they are, and what they value. What may be less obvious, is that each organisation also has its own culture, a brand created by values that are both expressed and unexpressed.

People reveal their values by how they behave and what they pay attention to. As a manager and business leader, you will project a 'brand' through the values you portray. Your behaviours reveal what's important to you, as well as what's important to your boss or your organisation. Your behaviours demonstrate your values. If you are in a position of power and authority, you will be watched in everything you do and everything you say. What you like and don't like will be noticed. People will consciously and unconsciously be adapting their behaviour to match yours in order to fit in. Since people will match both the good and the bad, so what key messages do you want to send out? Do people hear you encouraging them to consider their own needs as well as the business needs? Or do they just hear you talking about the business needs? Is that OK for you? Is your organisation a culture or a business where long hours are required and that's what people sign up for?

Many people need to feel they belong. Belonging to an organisation they can identify with and feel proud of working for, fulfills that need. An organisational brand that works for

one person may not work for another, however. This need
for belonging to something more than one's self seems to be
growing more important. According to André Gorz, this need
to feel part of a membership to some wider community or
corporate culture gives people a sense of security.

*The firm offers them the kind of security [which] monastic
orders, sects and work communities provide. It asks them to
give up everything – to give up any form of allegiance, personal
interests and even their personal lives – in order to give
themselves body and soul to the company, which in exchange
will provide them with an identity, a place, a personality and a
job they can be proud of.*
Andre Gorz – Reclaiming Work Policy Press 1999

For example, Microsoft's strategy was to actively recruit personalities that will fit in with their culture. They look for commitment, vigour, ability to handle ambiguity, a desire to be the best, to be stretched and a willingness to work long hours. It is known and accepted that the bottom 5% of performers are managed out each year. Microsoft know they are excluding certain portions of the workforce and are selective about who they recruit. They discount 1000s in the recruitment process and are happy for people to move on when their life circumstances and values change. They are not offering loyalty but they do pay higher salaries.

Other cultures have other values. BP is traditionally more paternalistic. They have traditionally recruited good people and want to keep them for life and move them around the organisation – 'lifers' as they call them. They want them to have BP 'DNA'.

In the book 'Good to Great', Jim Collins cites the Gillette senior management team as 'very close'. They are a hard-working team who debate ruthlessly but come out united and supportive of whatever is agreed, and they work a standard week with good work/life balance.

All of these typify very successful businesses with distinct brands. There will be both happy people and unhappy people in them. It just depends on whether the brand suits you and your values.

CHOOSING the Brand that Suits You

What excites you and motivates you about working and what puts you off? Have you noticed what no longer excites and motivates you as you have changed and grown over the years? If your values are changing and you're in an organisation that insists on their 'pound of flesh' you may not want to keep up the frenetic pace, especially if your end-date for your working life is changing. Or you may have the time, energy and drive to work and you want to be rewarded for that. Retirement used to mean 'not working for pay'. Now it means 'what amount of work do I need to do to support my lifestyle and those I'm responsible for'? So you need to choose an organisation that allows a different work pace or benefits to meet your needs.

Work/life balance improves when you get to know yourself better. Then you can choose what you want, as opposed to what others expect of you. When choosing whether or not to work for an organisation, you consider the whole package before making your decision. The interest in the culture of that organisation, their brand, has become much more important. Are they a 'good' employer? Do they fit with me and my values? Are they 'cool' to work for? Do they reflect who I am? Or am I embarrassed about working for them?

You begin to have expectations of the organisation and create an ideal. As thinking and expectations change, you become more sophisticated. How do you fit with your organisation? Are they offering what you want? Do they fit with your values?

EXERCISE

Exploring your values at work

First, work out the things that are important to you.

- On Post-it™ notes, write down as many answers to the following questions as you can think of (one answer per Post-it™). Be thorough!

Q. What is important to you in your working life?
Q. What adds to your work life?
Q. What do you enjoy? What gives you energy? What motivates you?

- Spread them out and decide which ones you could live without and which you couldn't live without.
- Out of the ones that you couldn't live without which one is most important?
- Take that one and compare it to each of the others and say to yourself: If I had to choose, which one would I keep. This will be your No 1 value about work.
- Take the next most important one and repeat the exercise until you have the second most important value.
- Repeat until you have 7 values.

These are the things that you need to be looking for in work. If you are not getting the top 3 or 4 met over a period of time, then you will start to feel a sense of dissatisfaction or frustration.

Then, think of all the things that drain you:

Q. What don't you like?

Q. What drains you?

Q. What is dull, boring and deflating?

The things that you don't like can be compared and ranked in
a similar way. Consider how much of these you are willing to
manage in your work. What is the threshold, that when reached,
may destroy the balance of enjoyment in your work no matter
how many of your desirable values are being met?

EXAMPLE

Shall I stay or shall I go?

A Senior Manager had worked five months for a UK-owned global retailer when she began questioning whether it was the right fit. She had previously worked for an American company in various countries throughout Asia and the States. Through her coaching, she re-assessed and ranked the elements she valued in her work. She valued: 'getting results, personal satisfaction, having responsibility, knowing how things ticked, completing and finishing things'. She didn't like: 'bullying, intimidation, being ridiculed in public, cliques, lack of vision, and vague objectives'.

For four months, she had been working on a very poorly managed research project that was not due to deliver results for some time. Because several of her key work values were not being met, she felt frustrated. Even worse, her boss seemed weak and lacked respect in this macho organisation where intimidation and bullying were the norm. So, after completing her assessment, it was not surprising that she felt adamant that this new organisation did not fit for her. She was going to think about her next move.

However, on questioning, she reflected that she was on secondment so this frustrating period with lack of job satisfaction and poor management would end in a couple of months. Then she would be given a post where she was part of an operations team who could produce results more quickly. She decided to stay with the new company despite being offered a more senior position with her old company.

Return on investment

This one coaching session alone saved the company a huge amount of money and time in not having to rehire if this lady left. She is still with the company three years later, adding a huge amount of value to the business.

"Men weary as much of not doing the things they want to do as of doing the things they do not want to do."
Eric Hoffer

SETTING Your Boundaries

Having boundaries simply means being clear about what is really important to you. Once you have clarity about what matters and what you want, you know where to draw the line. Boundaries refer to your deepest values about honesty, trust, respect, and regard, as well as to more practical aspects of your personal space, the limits of your time, personal remarks, etc. If you are not clear, then anyone with stronger demands or a more compelling argument, vision, plan, goal, idea, or request can take the lead over your work and your life.

The Price of No Boundaries
"I've been down the road of working all the hours God sends. I worked late into the evening, plus the occasional early morning in an attempt to keep up with the workload. I used weekends just to recover and get ready for the demands of the week again. Social activities got curtailed as they were too exhausting for my worn-out state. Eventually I ended up taking time off work to sort my head out. Finally I realised that if I didn't set boundaries, no-one else would!"

When you are clear about what is important to you, you can say 'no' with integrity. If asked, you can articulate your reasons, and feel confident that you are doing what's best for you, your family and your organisation. Building a clear picture of what will give you that internal sense of satisfying achievement and enjoyment will make all the difference.

"That is our chief bane, that we live not according to the light of reason, but after the fashion of others."
Seneca, Roman Philosopher & Dramatist, 65 A.D

Managing MEETINGS

Set boundaries about meetings!

Have you ever come out of a meeting and felt it was a waste of time? Have you heard about 'working smarter' but you're still wondering what that means? Have you ever booked meetings into your diary without asking about the purpose or content? Often people assume that they are invited to meetings because their contribution is required. They may even feel flattered and feel that being included signifies their high-level purpose. Then they arrive at the meeting and discover that other people haven't turned up because they had more important things to do. As they crawl through a tedious and frustrating agenda, they imagine how they could have made a better use of their time, and leave feeling very dissatisfied.

Challenge the need for your attendance at a meeting! Being clear about your boundaries will help increase productivity. Ask these pertinent questions:

- What is the purpose of this meeting?
- What is my role? What is my expected contribution? Do you really need me there? What would happen if I wasn't there?
- Who else will be going? Why? What are their roles and expected contribution?
- What is the expected outcome? Is it for understanding? To make decisions? To give opinions?
- What are people's expectations of the meeting, behaviours, commitment?
- How long will the meeting be? Will it end on time?

- Ask for inputs that outline the purpose, expected decisions, key issues, options for resolution. Explain these are needed to allow you the time to give your considered opinion.
- Ask for a review of the effectiveness of the meeting. What went well? What didn't? What can you all learn about making the meetings more effective and satisfying?

When you start asking these questions, everyone will start thinking more clearly. There may be a little resistance or fobbing off. People may not like being asked these questions, particularly if they haven't thought it through themselves. So you may need to gently coach them.

- Ask them the questions above and use a softer voice tone to convey curiosity and not blame or judgement.
- Let them know that you are re-evaluating the meetings that you go to so you can be more focused and productive.
- Let them know you are doing this with all meetings so it isn't directed at them.
- If you have any templates for your own meetings, share this with them so they can see the thinking process you go through.

Please also look at chapter three for tips on influencing and managing your time.

PASSION Killers

Passion Killers v Passion Enhancers

Fact: Human beings like to be social with other humans. People go for coffee or lunch to catch up with friends to find out what's happening in their lives. At work we do the same with our colleagues. It's a little bit of 'play' time during the day where you can have a laugh which helps reduce tension and stress and gives you a break from work. Unfortunately, many people get so caught up in the important and varied actions of everyday life, they forget what 'play' even is. What is the difference between Action Time and Play Time?

Action Time: An arranged meeting has **major decision topics** for one or all of the participants. Meetings mean action, doing, discussing or evaluating important decisions in your business or personal life.

Play Time: 'Catch up' has **NO major decision topics** for any of the participants. 'Catch up' means play, rest, relaxation, smiles, laughs, some unwind time...and no major decision topics.

A mistake one client used to make with the managers he worked with, was to confuse these two. He had always operated in a fast-paced, get-it-done environment. Occasionally, some of the team would invite him to join them for lunch. He knew they just wanted to take a 45-minute break from work, get recharged and come back in ready to make things happen. But he would always go with an agenda.

He would listen to them talk about their kids, football or the holiday they were planning. Then, at what he thought was an appropriate time, he would say, "Oh, by the way, Colin, how did the meeting with the MD go?" or "Chris, how did the sales figures look midweek?" Instantaneously you could see the whole complexion of that lunch change. They didn't have a very relaxing lunch and he didn't have a very good meeting. And ... they stopped asking him to lunch!

Now he has learned to identify whether it is a meeting he wants or social catch-up time. That way nobody has to sit on the edge of their mental seat waiting for the moment when he switches into work mode while they're eating.

What do you do if someone else crosses boundaries? Here are some ideas, you may be able to think of more:

- Change the subject.
- Say you'll come and see them later.
- Ask if you can talk about this after lunch.
- Avoid eye contact.
- Tell them you haven't got that information in your head right now.
- Be silent – chew your food 20 times – it's good for your digestion!

SETTING Family Boundaries

Setting boundaries with your family

When your work/life balance is set at the right level, the time you have for your family and friends will be enough to nourish everyone's needs. When you are off-kilter, they will complain, demand more of your time, feel neglected and start doing their best to distract you and capture your attention. Setting boundaries with loved ones cannot be rigid, because needs change as life happens.

Communication and negotiation are the key words here. If you are never at home, it is unfair to expect everyone to cut you slack indefinitely. There may be stressful times at work, and there may be stressful events happening on the home front. Clear communication and understanding of everyone's needs and wants must be negotiated. The price of not setting the right boundaries may lead to an increase in domestic tension. For some partners, working longer hours serves as the perfect way to avoid the issue, but that's no solution.

BOGOF!

The Buy One Get One free offer ... is now over

In the past, when an organisation employed a person (usually a man) they also got one free (normally a woman). The wife at home managed all the domestic and family responsibilities, allowing the man to focus entirely on paid work for the organisation. Now, many households cannot afford to live without two incomes. According to the Department for Work and Pensions 2001, 46% of the workforce is female, and 80% of the workforce growth is predicted to be women.

The male breadwinner model has moved on. This means changes in roles for everyone in the family. Expectations must be managed differently. Agreements need to be made that work for all involved. A new balance has to be established. These issues will not disappear or go back to how things used to be. Companies that are still stuck in the old breadwinner age will suffer, because demographics indicate the new labour market is different – older, more female, more ethnically diverse. With more women working, there's no-one at home anymore. Childcare and the handling of domestic needs are now a prominent issue of employment packages.

ASSESSING your Changing Needs

People have different needs at different times of life. The younger working population seek good pay and career opportunities and are willing to work long hours for them. They may also enjoy more work-related social activities. Parents usually need to reduce their working hours to bring up young children. Some people may wish to retrain, acquire new skills or take a sabbatical. Older workers may prefer a gradual exit from their careers as opposed to simply stopping work on a given day. Now it is as important to assess your 'lifetime' work/life balance as much as your weekly balance. Here are some great questions to get you thinking:

- What stage of life are you and people around you in now?
- Has anything changed over the previous months/ years?
- What do you expect from your partner? Has this changed?
- What do they expect from you? Has this changed?
- What roles have you consciously or unconsciously put each other in?
- What balance do you need over the next 12 – 24 months?
- What would you like to stay the same and what would you like to shift?

Discuss these questions with your loved ones. Once you have agreed on a new balance, remember that it will take some time and practice to change the habitual ways you operate. You can know something intellectually, but remembering to do it is another story. To help this process along, get your loved ones to help you manage it by asking questions like:

- What do you want me to do if you overstep this boundary or break this new rule?
- How can I best handle this with you?

"The perils of overwork are slight compared with the dangers of inactivity."
Thomas A. Edison

EXAMPLE

Managing the Nanny

A working mother with a considerable international role, needed to find better ways to manage her home life. With coaching, she carefully re-assessed what she expected of her husband, her nanny and herself, each morning and evening. After she thought this through in detail, she planned how she was going to communicate this to each person:

- What I want the nanny to do/not do as I enter the house.
- What I expect my husband to do/not do to and why.
- How to tell the nanny there's no time to chit-chat in the morning or evening.
- Instead they would spend time each Wednesday evening catching up.
- What information I want from the nanny each evening regarding the children e.g. their health, what they'd done and eaten etc.

MANAGING your Energy

Making good decisions requires a clear head. A tired, exhausted brain will not make decisions expediently. Just ticking things off your 'To Do' list may not be as efficient as you think. Managing your energy means doing the things that energise you. When you work on what inspires you, you'll unleash more energy to make your life work for you. Then you'll not only make better decisions but be able to implement them.

Why is it important to manage your energy?

Managing your energy means that you have the mental power to take control of your situation, to take that step back, to get off the hamster wheel and THINK. 'Does this fit with what I want? If I do or say this, is it in alignment with what I've decided to do differently?' Having energy means you have the reserves to resist the temptations to fall back into your old patterns. You'll have the energy it takes to stop others and challenge their thinking.

Remember, to have work/life balance, be ruthless about:

- Protecting your energy
- Defending your boundaries

"Life, if thou knowest how to use it, is long enough."
Seneca, Roman Philosopher & Dramatist, 65 A.D

EXERCISE

You only live once – be ruthless with your energy!!!

- Review your to-do list and delete unnecessary tasks.
- Reschedule or delay some tasks so they don't interfere with major projects.
- Delegate tasks to others, especially if they can do them better or faster.
- Create shortcuts, such as templates for client reports, to cut the time needed for repetitive tasks.
- Before you go home each day, write down the six most important things you need to do the next day.
- Schedule the most important things first.
- Be realistic about how long things take.
- Allow time for the unexpected.
- Don't waste the first hour of the day, when you're freshest.
- Never check email in the morning – use those early and fresh hours to tackle your most important projects.
- Turn off your Blackberry and phone – set and defend your boundaries

Please see more tips in chapter three.

The Grapes of Wrath

Does Conflict Enable or Block Progress?

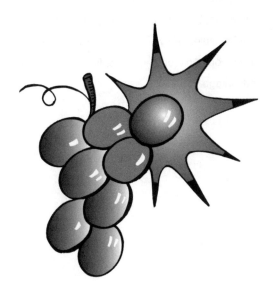

by Maggie Rose

The GRAPES of Wrath

Handling Unhelpful Conflict in Business

Conflict gets bad press in the business world. Agreement, co-operation, compliance and commitment are usually preferred. But healthy conflict forms an essential part of the creative process. How do you measure the costs and benefits of conflict? Can you afford not to face and deal with the unhelpful conflicts that block progress? How can you manage the type of positive conflict that enables productivity? What can you do when entrenched arguments slow down the decision-making process, and differences stifle open communication? When it becomes more important to be right, than to move forward, everyone suffers. In order to resolve conflict, you need clarity about what is most important, you need tools to move beyond the impasse, and you need to know the right questions to ask. Then you can stop seeing conflict as a threat and turn it to your advantage.

The KEY to Survival

What do you think are the characteristics for survival in business?

- Intelligence?
- Strength?
- The ability to adapt?

Charles Darwin, the father of the theory of evolution of the species, said the essential key to his concept of 'survival of the fittest' was adaptability. His extensive research revealed that all living things struggle unceasingly to survive. It is the organism's response to changes in its environment that makes all the difference. In the jungle of the work place, there are many similarities! Adapting to change is not a one-time event. Change must be continuous. You need to keep on adapting every time you learn something new, every time you try something new, every time you expose yourself to a new place, a new person, a new idea. The person who survives, learns and adapts continuously.

ENABLING the Right Sort of Conflict

How can you encourage the right sort of conflict in business relationships? Some leaders actively create discord by putting people in situations, particular roles, relationships or by making them accountable for particular change. They are probably seeking to encourage creativity, to strengthen initiative, and to develop capabilities. When their positive purpose is well understood and the process is well managed, it works. People grow, develop and achieve. When their intention is unclear or misunderstood however, the danger is that the well intentioned conflict tips over to become unwelcome interference. Whenever conflict blocks instead of enabling, productivity diminishes, business results are compromised and individual confidence and commitment are at stake. When the scales have tipped, it's time to change your focus and learn how to handle unhelpful conflict.

"A good manager doesn't try to eliminate conflict; he tries to keep it from wasting the energies of his people. If you're the boss and your people fight you openly when they think that you are wrong – that's healthy."
Robert Townsend

SYMPTOMS of Unhelpful Conflict

- It's more important to be right than to move forward
- Subordinates get caught in bosses' differences
- Difficulties arise between central functions and lines of business
- Slow and tortuous decision-making processes
- Inconsistency or lack of understanding
- Diversity of opinion is perceived as a threat
- Suppressed anger behind politically correct, polite communication
- Talented people question their commitment to the business
- Progress slows due to passive resistance
- Over escalation of decision-making

Of course, some people seem to thrive on conflict. When they engage in conflict just for the sake of conflict, however, they often get labelled as having 'style issues'. They don't rise in the company, because they are seen as having an inability to bring others with them – an essential leadership skill.

EXAMPLE

Looking for Conflict

Rachel had a phenomenal education incorporating scholarships, and a variety of accolades, including Harvard. The organisation that recruited her, recognised her incredible intelligence as well as her individual talent. They wanted to bring some new thinking to the way they operated. Rachel felt very excited about the opportunity to take this business forward. Her style of approaching this challenge was to look for conflict with people. Although she wanted mutual respect in working relationships, she engaged in a way to test others. Through challenge and conflict she would judge whether they were a valuable colleague and worthy of respect. She positively thrived off the intellectual challenge that someone would give her. The conflict energised her thinking. Her positive purpose was to improve the quality of thinking she could contribute to the organisation.

Unfortunately, her approach alienated her colleagues. Wishing to avoid conflict and judgement, they withheld their thinking. Her behaviour appeared negative and destructive, despite the positive intention behind it. Rachel wanted to create a better solution and bring others with her.

To do what she *really* wanted and avoid the conflict she had created, she needed to:

- be clear with herself and others on these values
- adopt behaviour that demonstrated those values to others
- change her attitude from searching for detailed fault-finding to focusing on the effect she wished to create in the working relationship

CONFLICT in Different Career Phases

Conflict will always be a feature of life. The skill of managing conflict is therefore worth mastering. This pays off both in business and at home. Some organisations believe a culture of engaging in conflict is laudable. They encourage conflict as an important phase in early career. Those seen to 'strut their stuff' are often viewed as people with potential. However, once they reach middle / senior management, a change happens in how individuals are viewed. You are no longer valued as an asset when seen as someone constantly seeking a fight. Different capabilities become valued: the quality of thought that improves the way the business operates as well as the ability to bring people with you: direct reports, peers, bosses stakeholders and shareholders. Creating unhelpful conflict limits the development of those essential leadership capabilities.

"In dwelling, live close to the ground.
In thinking, keep to the simple.
In conflict, be fair and generous.
In governing, don't try to control.
In work, do what you enjoy.
In family life, be completely present."
Tao Te Ching

The WILL to Handle Conflict

Why bother?

The ability to handle conflict is a skill that can be learned BUT only if there's the 'will' to do so. It's not enough to just have the will to learn the skill. What's needed is the will to handle and resolve the conflict. Asking the right sort of questions can help increase the motivation to tackle and resolve unhelpful conflicts.

There's an appropriate idiom concerning aptitude or 'will':

You can take a horse to water but you can't make it drink.

I'd like to add:

Yes, but you can put salt in its oats!

If there isn't the will, you will never find the way. If you are tempted to do nothing, just make sure you can live with the ramifications. What will be the cost of perpetuating this conflict: for yourself, for others and for the whole organisation? Ask yourself, "What if you do nothing – what will be the effect twelve months from now?" When you become aware of the costs to you, you might start feeling thirsty to do something about it.

ome BENEFITS of Resolving Conflict

- Energy focused on serving the customer
- Alignment as a team to succeed in the market
- Removing interference that limits performance
- Joint decision-making accelerated
- Harnessing the strengths of diversity
- Relationships functioning well, generating trust and loyalty
- Increased personal success and enhanced reputation
- People feel good about coming to work
- Less stress-induced illness / absence

ASSESS the Worth

Assess the Worth of Handling Conflict

So, what's in it for you to handle and resolve unhelpful conflict? Is making the change *really* worth the effort? If you don't believe it's worth your effort, then why would you have the will to resolve it? The familiar cost/benefit analysis can help you assess that worth. Most people in business have used this tool in some context. By assessing the two dimensions of cost and benefit for a proposed change – personal or professional – you can quickly and easily establish the conscious pros and cons. The adapted version that follows adds some spice to that rational thought. It will flush out any underlying unconscious or unspoken objections that need to be recognised. You will then have a complete picture of data to comprehensively help you assess whether it is *worth* handling and resolving the conflict.

"I always cheer up immensely if an attack is particularly wounding because I think, well, if they attack one personally, it means they have not a single political argument left."
Margaret Thatcher

EXERCISE

Cost / Benefit Analysis

Simply fill in the answers in the boxes below, while thinking of
a specific relationship with another individual with whom you
would like to resolve conflict and increase productivity.

What is the **cost** of changing your approach?	What is the **benefit** of changing your approach?
What is the **benefit** of NOT changing your approach?	What is the **cost** of NOT changing your approach?

By separating out the four dimensions of cost and benefit, it's
easy to assess the worth of resolving the conflict. To make
the most of the process, be your own devil's advocate and
make sure you've given the best and most complete answers
possible.

EXAMPLE

Disillusioned with the Boss

As IT Director with responsibility for the global strategy of a fast growing business, Joe had a conflict in his business relationship with the boss. His boss oversaw the IT function as part of his multiple accountabilities, but he appeared disinterested in that function. As a result, Joe became disillusioned, thinking that his boss was not supporting him, nor contributing to his thinking. He couldn't change his boss, nor his boss's accountabilities. But he could change how he chose to manage that relationship. Joe did a cost/benefit analysis to assess whether he was willing to resolve the passive resistance in their relationship.

What is the **cost** of changing your approach?	What is the **benefit** of changing your approach?
· *It's going to take time, thought and planned action to engage my boss in addition to getting on with my 'day' job* · *It might not work*	· *My ideas will be heard by my peers and boss* · *To build productivity in our working relationship* · *To enjoy coming to work* · *To neutralise the negative effect the working relationship is having on me* · *To stop whinging at home*
What is the **benefit** of NOT changing your approach?	What is the **cost** of NOT changing your approach?
· *Continued sympathy of others* · *Less hassle?*	· *Career progression slowing down* · *Being seen as not coping with managing this person* · *Performance review could be less than I deserve* · *Bonus / salary review could be affected*

Through analysing both costs and benefits, Joe realised the bigger picture. Although he thought he was weighing up whether he wanted to handle and resolve the conflict itself, it was much more than that. He realised he needed to make a decision about his reputation in the business. Because of this conflict, questions were likely to be raised about his capability to manage this particular senior individual.

The data showed him he had a positive opportunity to develop his capability in managing relationships and being seen to do so.

Joe decided to take control.

He scheduled time with his boss. Time where they could work on useful business issues together. Time where he got his boss out of the office. Time where they could talk naturally and with ease. Their relationship began to improve.

MEASURING the Opportunity

There's an old adage: *'If you can't measure it you can't manage it'*. In order to ensure that an initiative is worth pursuing or *'the juice is worth the squeeze,'* it is worth measuring the status quo at the outset. You need to be able to measure a result that has meaning for you. What is the financial cost of the conflict you are experiencing? For most people in business, even an estimate of financial cost is certainly a measure that gives definite meaning.

EXERCISE

Measuring the Conflict

Think about a business relationship with another individual where you currently have conflict and would like to increase productivity. Conflict acts as interference: interference limits productivity. By measuring that interference you will be able to quantify cost now and quantify change in the future.

| 0 | 1 | 2 | 3 | 4 | 5 | 6 | 7 | 8 | 9 | 10 |

Low   High

1. What is the cost of this conflict now? On the scale [where 0 is no belief and 10 is absolute belief] score the following:

- Your belief in the **POTENTIAL** of that relationship
- Your opinion of where that relationship is currently **OPERATING** relative to the **POTENTIAL**

For example:

2. Take the score of your belief in the **potential** of that relationship. What is your evidence? What supports your belief? How do you know that's true? Jot these thoughts down.

3. Take the score of where the relationship is currently **operating**. What's your evidence for that? What supports that belief? How do you know that's true? Jot down these thoughts, too.

4. You can now define the gap. You have two lists of supporting evidence to help you. When you compare the two lists, what's the gap? What stops the possible potential being realised today? Is there:

- Lack of clarity?
- Unfamiliarity?
- Unhelpful conflict?

These are typical factors.

5. What's the gap you see from comparing your two lists – this is the gap in your relationship? Make a note of this for yourself.

6. What needs to happen to close this gap? What has to be true? How could this potential be realised? Make an action list.

EXAMPLE

Measuring Conflict

An entrepreneurial technology driven enterprise had a Board comprised of seven highly paid, highly capable individuals. The CEO was experiencing conflict with her team. Talking to her and using the given scale, she measured her belief in their combined potential as 10. The evidence and beliefs that supported that were:

- Belief in the commitment and capability of individuals to work hard and find best business solutions
- Recognition of the diversity of experience in the team which added strength
- Respect for her own capability to find the best route for future business success

And where were they **operating**? At 5 = just half their potential. Quite a gap. And what evidence and beliefs supported that?

- Inconsistency of understanding the vision of the business
- In day-to-day meetings, diversity of approach and perspective being seen and treated as a threat
- The team not knowing each other as human beings
- Over-escalation of issues to the leader
- Slow decision-making
- Progress and action being held back through passive resistance

How could the CEO realise potential and resolve unhelpful conflict? She decided to:

- *Jointly* create and then unite her team in a common vision
- Understand the strength of the diversity around the table and how to capitalise on that asset
- Spend time getting to know one another
- Devolve responsibility of the team dynamic to be held by *everyone*, not simply directed at or expected *from* the leader
- Define what mattered to them as a team and understand how they needed to work together day-to-day to achieve this

These were highly paid, powerful senior leaders in industry. Each had leadership responsibility to take the teams' productivity forward and stop perpetuating unhelpful conflict.

If you added the collective remuneration of this Board, it amounts to £5 million. From the CEO's measurement, they were operating at half their potential! If equated to remuneration, this gap represented a cost of £2.5 million plus opportunity lost! In taking a baseline assessment and then recognising the gap from where they were operating they had an opportunity to realise their collective potential; an opportunity that could be measured and had meaning. Luckily this CEO recognised that opportunity and took action.

Through spending facilitated time together working on their team relationship as well as working on their operational and strategic tasks, the gap in performance closed. The commercial results for the organisation reflected their collective success by moving the business from one that was struggling to break even, to being an envied player in the technology sector. By the end of its third year of trading, the business was driving out increasing operating profit on a regular basis.

Although this measuring method relies on subjective assessment of the cost of conflict, by translating performance into financial cost, it not only grabs attention but has universal meaning. It is quick and simple to calculate and focuses attention on the remedy. It is not intended to be rigorous. It is intended to provide a useful indicator with measurement focused on the benefits to be gained by handling and resolving unhelpful conflict.

"There are no facts, only interpretations."
Nietzsche

SYMPTOM or Cause?

Conflict may be easy to recognise, but be wary of hidden underlying causes that may be even more important to address. Ponder this question: 'Is this a real conflict that needs directly addressing or could it be a signal that there's something else going on here?' If you did resolve this conflict would it simply reoccur in another guise, another time, another place? Sometimes these 'conflict dolphins' that keep popping their heads up above the water may not be the issue. Are the waves of conflict in this relationship repetitive? Are they increasing in size? If so, the problem may be in the seabed and *that's* what needs to be noticed, responded to and addressed. Examples might include:

- Role design
- Role fit
- Team structure
- Level of capability
- Unclear accountabilities

Treating the cause (not just the symptom)

Being buffeted by waves of perpetual conflict wears people down, erodes their energy, and depletes their emotional loyalty. There's nothing dignified about visible conflict that ultimately leaves individuals or the organisation in tatters. Individuals typically end up taking the greatest cost in reputation. Although harder to measure, the internal scars can feel like the aftermath of a tidal wave.

EXAMPLE

Deeper Causes for Conflict

Sally was Commercial Director of a manufacturing business.
She had been appointed into the organisation as an external
hire. She inherited her team of seven direct reports. After three
months, she had a good feel for her individual direct reports
and their capabilities. The ambitions of the organisation and
her goals within it were challenging. Current performance
was poor. There were pockets of conflict within the team.
She needed them to be aligned in order to win in the market.
Instead energy got wasted on conflict between themselves and
the rest of the business. She had a choice.

Plan A

To invest time, money, expertise and energy in identifying
and resolving all the different dimensions of the conflicts. This
appealed to her overriding belief that 'anything is possible'. She
wanted to give people the best chance. So this approach felt
compelling.

Plan B

To ask herself whether she had the right people in the team,
given the vision of the business, the strategy to achieve
that, the structure necessary to deliver that, and the current
operating performance. She needed to question whether she
believed, given developmental investment, they would make it?
Would they change enough in the time available?

She realised that despite her good intentions towards people,
deep down she believed that two of those team members would

not make it. The choice was clear: either change her belief, or change those two people.

Her conclusion: replace the two people, notice how conflict resolves as a result and then support any further needs with development investment. A combination of both Plan A and Plan B.

As a leader, she learned that if you don't believe something will happen or don't believe in somebody then that belief will overshadow any possibility of change.

Making your DECISION

So, if you have assessed your business relationship as less than optimal. If you've established measurement of the **potential** of that relationship versus where it is **operating**. If you have quantified the historic cost *and* you have comprehensively assessed the potential **costs** and **benefits** of making a change in that relationship, then you have all the data you need to analyse. It's decision time. How will you decide whether to handle your conflict or leave matters as they are?

There are two questions that need to be satisfied. Given all of your data:

- Is it possible?
- Is it worth it?

"The difference between 'involvement' and 'commitment'
is like an eggs-and-ham breakfast:
the chicken was 'involved' – the pig was 'committed'."
Unknown

The ART of the Possible

Some would say that anything's possible if you set your mind to it. *Reality* also needs to be considered. The reality of what you can control and what you can't must be assessed. What can you *really* control? And if you can't control it, what can you *influence*?

You can do something about both what you control and what you influence. Anything outside of that is 'bad lands'. What's the point of putting energy into worrying about, talking about, thinking about or getting into conflict about things that are outside of your control or influence? At the end of the day, each of us can only control ourselves. There are things in a business setting that will be outside of our control and influence. Spending time in those 'bad lands' is a waste and a distraction.

It's easy to find yourself wasting a lot of time, debating in your own mind and/or with others, why certain situations occur. For example, how is it that people can be given accountability for an area in which they have no interest, aptitude or capability? If you can't change the boss's accountabilities or role, this is 'bad lands'. Perhaps that decision was down to the CEO. It is out of your sphere of influence. But the sphere of influence you can control is powerful. You can:

- Influence the processes in the relationship
- Control your own perspective by looking at your boss as a resource and consider what assets your boss could bring: for example, the doorways that could open by virtue of his/her seniority

So, is it possible? When you accept what you can influence and control, the answer should be clear. If you are willing and motivated to handle and resolve the conflict, then it's time to think about 'how'.

"Face adversity promptly and without flinching and you will reduce its impact."
Winston S Churchill

BUILDING the Skills to Handle Conflict

Knowing that you're going to get the best return on investment from taking action on things you can control or influence, what you need are specific frameworks to help create conversations that will change the relationship. You will need to check your own clarity and integrity. You will need to maintain a balanced perspective, tempering any emotion that may get in the way of resolving that conflict. Preparation is vital! Then you can be in control of difficult conversations.

The Golden Rule

It is essential to have clarity and control within yourself BEFORE attempting to resolve a conflict with someone else. Often the conflict you experience in your own mind complicates what gets played out in relationships with others. You need to complete negotiations with yourself before you negotiate with others. That's the golden rule. You need to be clear in your own mind and well prepared for a conversation with others in order to resolve conflict.

No two conflict situations will be the same. Remember, especially when managing relationships, that everyone is unique. Therefore, every conflict situation will have its own unique qualities with different dynamics at play. People think differently, they speak differently, they focus on different aspects, they choose different objectives. Each conflict situation needs to be handled with care. Your knowledge and

"You must be the change you wish to see in the world."
Gandhi

experience of yourself and others are essential components in conflict resolution. You already have many skills you can build on, and it's possible to learn what to do when relationships are not working. Remember to celebrate the relationships that are working!

EXERCISE

Establishing Values: The skill of taking the high ground
People have different values in different contexts. Each set of values is specific to a particular context of your life. Test this out for yourself ...

- What's important to you in the context of your *professional working relationship* with your boss?
- What's important to you in the context of a *particular personal relationship*; for example, with your children / parents / loved ones?

Compare your answers – are they the same?

Perhaps the answers to the first question might look like:
- Support
- Challenge
- Co-operation

Perhaps the answers to the second question might look like:
- Unconditional love
- Laughter
- Honesty

It's very unlikely that 'unconditional love' would be very important to you in the context of your relationship with your boss!

The *professional working relationship* with your boss and a *particular personal relationship* are two different contexts in your life. It's therefore quite appropriate to think of them as separate.

SHIFTING Values re Time

As well as values being context specific, they are also specific
to particular times of life. What is important to many people
in their professional life during their early twenties, is deciding
their career path, establishing credibility and earning money.
During their thirties, it's usually about climbing the ladder of
success, ticking boxes. By their forties, the focus of importance
has shifted to the meaning of their professional contribution
and quality of life. Each phase of life has different values and
objectives that shift and evolve. It's easy to be out-of-date with
yourself. So the following process of identifying and ranking
your values needs regular attention. Updating what matters to
you is essential before handling any conflict. You will determine
what is non-negotiable as well as know where there is room for
flexibility. You will make better and more informed decisions.
You will handle and resolve conflict with clarity and integrity.

The following process will help you update yourself. It will
also give you an opportunity to negotiate with yourself before
engaging with others. You will be crystal clear on what matters
to you now.

EXERCISE

The Big Question of Values

Start by establishing the relevant Big Question. The Question needs to be relevant to the conflict you are wishing to resolve. Here are some examples:

- If your conflict is with the organisation, the Big Question could be:
  'What's important to me in the context of my professional life?'

- If your conflict is work / life balance, the Big Question could be:
  'What's important to me in my life in the next x years?'

- If your conflict is about career direction, the Big Question could be:
  'What's important to me about my future professional legacy?'

- If your conflict is with peers, the Big Question could be:
  'What's important to me in my working relationships?'

- If your conflict is with your spouse, the Big Question could be:
  'What's important to me in my marriage?'

1. Create the right Big Question for yourself that directly answers the conflict you are experiencing.

My Big Question is:

2. Brainstorm all the answers to your Big Question – in no particular order. You will probably have 7-12 answers

3. Now rank those factors, (1) being the most important. It can be tough to do this ranking as everything on the list will be important but force yourself to choose so that you create clarity. The ranking is not to eliminate any particular factors. It is to establish relative importance.

4. Next test the ranking through forced choice: Check each entry on the list testing (1) against (2), (2) against (3), (3) against (4) and so on. You are likely to find the list re-order itself. In the following example: David could 'spend time with his partner' and not 'fulfil his professional potential' or he could 'fulfil his professional potential' and not 'spend time with his partner.' This process tests whether you need to adjust your ranking and re-arrange your values. You are negotiating with yourself.

EXAMPLE

Is this the right career opportunity for me?

David worked in an organisation where it was usual for the senior leaders to dictate an individual's next career move. Individuals were invited to take on particular roles rather than apply for roles available. David had been presented with a career opportunity. He was unsure whether the role was right for him in the context of his total life balance. Working through the process to define what was important to him, here's the initial list, in ranked order, that he created, and his revised list:

What's Important To Me In My Life In The Next 5 Years?
1. Spending time with my partner
2. Fulfilling my professional potential
3. Being fit for life
4. Supporting my partner in career & life objectives
5. Stretching and educating myself professionally
6. Financial security for my family
7. Travel
8. Helping my kids achieve what they want
9. Personal time to pursue my hobbies
10. Maintaining contact with extended family

What's Important To Me In My Life In The Next 5 Years? (Revised List)

(Original ranking is shown in brackets [ ] so that you can clearly see the movement.)
1. [3] Being fit for life
2. [6] Financial security for my family
3. [1] Spending time with my partner
4. [2] Fulfilling my professional potential

5. [5]   Stretching and educating myself professionally

6. [4]   Supporting my partner in career & life objectives

7. [8]   Helping my kids achieve what they want

8. [7]   Travel

9. [10] Maintaining contact with extended family

10. [9] Personal time to pursue my hobbies

This exploration made David aware of the great conflict he had between the priorities of family commitment and professional demands. Working through this process enabled him to update himself, gaining clarity to make the right decision for himself, his family and his career.

A helpful tip: you might write each of the factors onto separate Post-it™ notes so you can move them around a table, like playing cards, as you test the ranking. Sometimes it helps to have someone read the list to you so that you can concentrate on carefully assessing which value is most important.

> *"They say that time changes things,*
> *but you actually have to change them yourself."*
> Andy Warhol

CREATING Joint Values

Have you ever been in the situation where, at the outset of a working relationship, the two people 'sitting at the table' had very different 'hidden' agendas? This is common. Using the 'Big Question Values Process' can be enormously powerful at the outset of working with colleagues. By thoroughly listing Values together, and then prioritising them, the hidden agendas surface. Then it is easier to negotiate and reach agreed joint outcomes for the situation you are facing or the specific task you are managing. Once you have identified your joint Values in order of importance, you can work down from the highest point of agreement to whatever level of detail you need, in order to set specific tasks. The Values become a framework for working together day-to-day, as well as your long-term professional relationship.

"If you have always done it that way,
it is probably wrong."
Charles Kettering

MANAGING Behaviours

The Skill Of Creating Clear Contracts

Research shows that people have such different patterns
of behaviour and such different values, that they are like
computers all running completely different operating systems
with incompatible software. Yet most people operate as if
everyone thinks the same and will therefore behave accordingly.
That diversity of thinking, different styles of decision-making,
opinion, beliefs, styles of communication, ways of working
– all commonly result in misunderstanding and conflict. Many
people scratch their heads and look mystified when others react
differently, or misunderstand. In fact, different backgrounds,
experiences, behaviours, patterns of thinking and style, are both
a blessing and a curse.

The human condition is to make meaning of others' behaviours.
We make our own interpretation based on our own patterns.
However, others' behaviour may have different intended
meaning from our interpretation. Engaging in mind-reading, and
in particular making negative assumptions in that mind-reading,
is the beginning of misunderstanding and unhelpful conflict.
For example, take the quality of 'support'. Two different people
might interpret that same quality in very different ways. One
individual might leave you alone believing that by giving you
space and time they were being very supportive; another might
proactively offer you lots of solutions believing that they were
offering you support through practical help. These are both
valid and yet entirely different behavioural interpretations for
the quality of 'support' in a professional working relationship.
One of these might work for you. Neither might work! It can
be extremely useful to specifically define and contract helpful

behaviours with colleagues. You then understand how to best engage in your professional day-to-day life. Through the following process you will be able to inform your colleagues how to get the best from you and through that conversation, ask how you can best give of yourself.

EXERCISE

2 X 2 Quadrant

Take a look at the 2 x 2 below.

	High Challenge Low Support	High Challenge High Support
	Low Challenge Low Support	Low Challenge High Support

CHALLENGE (HIGH / LOW)

SUPPORT (LOW / HIGH)

Support and **Challenge** are two factors that are central to professional working relationships. The type of **support** and **challenge** you might want will vary depending on the context of your professional relationship and your needs. The type of **challenge** and **support** you get will vary depending on the individual and their interpretation.

1. Take a moment to define what 'support' and 'challenge' mean to you in a professional working relationship. You might like to think of it as teaching someone how they would demonstrate 'support' for you. For example, 'Keep me informed of current data you know will impact my accountabilities.' What would define 'support' for you? List those qualities.

2. What would define 'challenge?' List those qualities.

3. Now think about the important relationships in your professional life. You could take your peer group or direct reports as a team or, alternatively, key individuals. On the blank grid, plot where your current relationship with them sits. Review each individual against your definitions of both 'support' and challenge' to plot them in the right place individually and relative to one another.

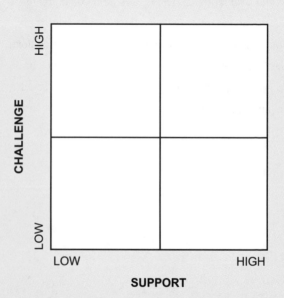

This process is incredibly effective to support the development of inter-cultural professional relationships. Different cultures bring about another level of complexity in human relationships beyond spoken language. Take the quality of 'challenge' as an example. In Asia challenge may be behaviourally unspoken and demonstrated through passive resistance which, for a colleague in the US could be interpreted as unsupportive – certainly not as helpfully challenging. In turn, the colleague from the US might behaviourally demonstrate challenge in open combat which the colleague in Asia might interpret as fundamentally disrespectful.

Understanding behaviours that positively demonstrate support and challenge in any professional relationship is a conversation worth having. By doing so, you will avoid misinterpretation, accelerate joint productivity and navigate conflict.

"Whosoever desires constant success
must change his conduct with the times."
Niccolo Machiavelli

EXAMPLE

A Problem of Diversity

Two very different individuals came together as CEO and COO through company acquisition. The CEO was Asian; the COO was European. For six months these two senior players battled out who was 'right'. Conflict reigned. Commercial results were unimpressive. Traction on integration was slow. An atmosphere of 'Them' and 'Us' was thriving.

Potentially they had a fabulous opportunity to share the different attributes that both individuals and both organisations had to offer. The integrity of their roles demanded this. It was their joint responsibility to drive out the value of the company merger.

Instead they invested a good deal of time and energy trying to change their colleagues to be the same as them or making negative meaning of each other's behaviour. It didn't occur to them to harness the their diversity of experience, behaviour and approaches. They were trying to get on with the job of taking the business forward but the conflicts arising out of diversity made progress painfully slow.

After they used the support and challenge quadrant, they were finally able to explore the diversity issue in a non-threatening way, and then discuss how to preserve the qualities that were useful. They now appreciated that they needed to harness diversity so that they could move forward.

They found what they both wanted was a colleague who would give them 'high challenge and high support'. What they were then able to do was to have a highly valuable conversation.

During the conversation they were able to give each other feedback on

- their experience of the working relationship now
- what defined the qualities of 'support' and 'challenge' for them individually
- what they wanted more of from their colleague by way of 'support' or 'challenge'
- what they wanted less of by way of 'support' or 'challenge'

By having these conversations they moved away from seeing the diversity between them as a threat and moved towards engaging effectively with each other.

Your ATTITUDE

The Skill Of Choosing Your Mindset

Things do go wrong. Difficulties arise. The mindset and approach you adopt has a great effect on how quickly you move through the problem and progress. It is not the failure itself that's the problem, it's how you deal with the failure that determines whether it's a failure or not. The failure itself has happened. That's a fact. It is in the past. You have a choice:

- to dwell on what has been, which you can neither change nor eradicate

- move on, being informed and learning from what has happened in the past

It's how you *relate* to what has happened that matters.

"People are always blaming their circumstances for what they are. I don't believe in circumstances. The people who get on in this world are the people who get up and look for the circumstances they want, and if they can't find them, make them."
George Bernard Shaw

EXAMPLE

Culture of blame

Roger was a leader of a senior marketing team. A perfectionist by nature, his preferred way of improving performance was to find all the holes in a situation. So his behaviour was very critical and constantly seeking to blame. He would ask 'What's wrong?' 'Whose fault is it?' 'Why did this happen?' 'How is this going to limit our objectives?' Everyone found this approach sapped their energy. As the leader of the team, however, he set the example of how to behave. His team were therefore adopting the same approach in managing their teams; both critical and blaming.

Over time, Roger started to wonder why people weren't coming to him with creative initiative to improve the business. The fact of the matter was that Roger had bred a culture of blame. It was his perfectionism that squashed creativity and bred fear, ultimately diminishing individual's contribution and confidence.

EXERCISE

It's Your Choice

Let's explore two different ways of looking at the same problem. Think of a conflict in any context that you have right now. Ask yourself:

- What's wrong?
- Whose fault is it?
- Who's to blame?
- Why did it happen?
- How will this limit your objectives?
- How will this limit your *joint* objectives?

Having answered those questions, what did you conclude? Now take the same situation and ask the following set of questions:

- What do you want?
- How did it happen?
- How can you learn from this?
- When have you faced something similar to this before and succeeded?
- How is this an opportunity?
- What is the next step?

The 'Blame' set of questions spirals into a negative powerless loop which results in blaming others, the circumstances or the world! The 'Outcome' set of questions lift you towards a more positive perspective, generating creative thinking, with some thoughts to move forward.

Even when reality does 'go wrong' the failure, or mistakes could be better perceived as learning. If you could talk to yourself in the past, what would you advise? Adopting such positive thinking is not about over-optimism, denial of reality or avoiding conflict. It is about refocusing on what you want at the highest level, taking responsibility, learning from mistakes and moving on.

"Show me someone who has done something worthwhile and I'll show you someone who has overcome adversity."
Lou Holtz

The LOCKED Horns of Conflict

Conflicts can be complex and deep, sometimes without the possibility of resolution. Sometimes simple tools of exploration can work wonders, but they are not panaceas. Measuring the cost of conflict on both the personal and the business level, it's clearly vital to handle and resolve conflicts whenever possible. When you can define the gap you want to close, when you muster the will to apply the required effort, then these useful frameworks and skills can provide you with powerful insights, and helpful perspectives. Solutions will become clear.

Each conflict is unique. Therefore each solution must be tailor made. Although these are just a small selection of tools, they have worked consistently to help people handle and resolve conflict in all kinds of situations. Whether the conflict involves the boss, teams or peers, the thinking needs to be clarified and well prepared before attempting any resolution. Then it is easier to create the opportunity to have constructive conversations. Although many people have a natural aptitude for diplomacy and conflict resolution, you can learn and develop the skills required for good, productive, professional relationships.

Resolving any 'interference' that gets in the way is essential to realising that potential. Unhelpful conflict in business is interference that diminishes vision and productivity. Managing and resolving conflict frees up creativity, deepens maturity and directs attention to commercial results.

Conclusion

Top tips to handle and resolve conflict

- Disagreement helps – it is a way of ultimately producing better solutions.

- Negotiate with yourself before negotiating with others. Such self-awareness is the foundation stone of emotional intelligence.

- Spend time and energy only on what you can control and influence. You are completely in control of how you behave. That's something you can change.

- Know precisely the effect you want to create in your relationship – your ideal as well as the minimum acceptable.

- Take the higher ground – you can lose a few battles but still win the war.

- Keep others sufficiently happy in order to win their longer-term collaboration. You'll get more out of people if you don't irritate them.

- Managing conflict is a process – there will be a reasonable route through. Demonstrate that hope as you jointly develop solutions.

Turning Juice into Wine

Create and Communicate the Mission of your Business

by Chris Southam

VISION for Success

Create & Communicate the Mission of your Business

It is important for leaders to understand the core purpose of their business. Being clear about what it is that they do and why they are doing it is fundamental to success. Confusion, low motivation and morale and inevitably a downturn in performance can happen if there is a lack of direction and purpose. A business will struggle to deliver objectives without clear vision. A good **Mission Statement** that incorporates the Vision can inspire and provide a clear direction for all of those in the organisation. The promises that it seeks to deliver, act as guidelines to each and every person, in every role. It takes clarity of thought, time, effort and planning to create and communicate a Vision; can you afford the costs of not doing so?

The Key Business Challenge

As a Leader, how can you build a Vision that has real meaning for your organisation? How can you communicate that purpose to your people through a Mission Statement? How can you inspire buy-in from everyone so that they represent and deliver it? You may have come across Mission Statements that sound aspiring but do not bear any relationship to what the company is about. Over the last fifteen years, a whole industry has grown up around helping companies to articulate their Vision into Mission Statements. Often the process is lengthy, expensive, with the final result not reflecting the reality of the business. This chapter explores techniques for constructing such a statement with clarity, simplicity and ownership.

A clear Vision articulated in a well-formed Mission Statement is powerful. Groups and organisations find that having a clear slogan increases motivation, loyalty and the cohesion of the workforce. What is less well known is that having such a clear sense of Vision and Mission also helps to point the way forward for individuals too. A good Mission Statement provides a framework of simplicity that can facilitate breakthrough solutions.

Mission Statements – Who Needs Them?

When could a business benefit from having a clear, uniform understanding of what it is they do? Identifying the core purpose of a company is often not as easy as it sounds. Especially after mergers and acquisitions, many companies struggle to clarify exactly what their unifying principles are. What do they stand for? What is their purpose? What are they producing? The need to understand a core purpose can be driven by:

- **Start-up** – new businesses need to be clear about what they are doing and who are they doing it for
- **Crisis** – under-performing businesses need to re-evaluate their core purpose and direction
- **Growth** – growing businesses need to understand what they must do to sustain and further improve their position
- **Innovation** – changes in the market or personal direction can mean it's time to refresh a vision

"It's not what the vision is, it's what the vision does."
Peter Senge

KEEP it Simple

If a business is new, under-performing, or subject to market or economic influences, it is necessary to really understand what the business is about, who it serves and how it should be run. Vision and Mission statements greatly facilitate this process of understanding. They provide a simple statement of the true aspiration and direction of the business. They can be one sentence or a group of statements that reflect the intent. The key to their success is simplicity and a 'back to basics' approach.

There are numerous examples of both good and not so good mission statements. Some of the better ones include:

'Solve complex network computing problems for governments, enterprises and service providers'
Sun Micro Systems

'The undisputed leader in world travel.'
British Airways 1997

'Every Little Helps'
Tesco

"Vision without action is a dream.
Action without Vision is simply passing the time.
Action with Vision is making a positive difference."
Joel Barker

When constructing a Mission statement, simple language is more important than expressing ideas with politically correct jargon. You may have come across Mission Statements that resemble the following parody of 'management speak'.

'Our mission is to continue to continually leverage other's market-driven catalysts for change so that we may endeavour to collaboratively network unique services to set us apart from the competition.'
Mission statement generator - Dilbert.com

"Capital isn't scarce. Vision is."
Michael Milken

EXERCISE

Six steps to achieving clarity

No matter what needs drive your Vision building, here are the specific points that will always require attention. Through careful observation, it's possible to get that clarity, simplicity and ownership that you need. It's as important to recognise the danger signals of your business, as it is to pay attention to the desires.

1. Listen to your customers - make sure you use the data of your customer feedback mechanisms to inform your sense of direction. Successful businesses give customers what they want and in some cases what they didn't even realise they wanted. Listening to what your customers tell you will help you deliver their desires.

2. Listen to your people - it is often the people in your organisation who are closest to the customers. They can often see opportunities and also help provide solutions to everyday challenges.

3. Get your top team round the table - this is the fastest way to create a fully integrated and 'signed up' to sense of purpose. Clarity must start with those people who are leading the business.

"It's a poor sort of memory that only works backwards."
Lewis Carroll

4. Review and value the history of your business
- many large organisations value their history and
look to it to provide a sense of future. The Disney
Corporation's Orientation programmes take new
people with them to their future by exploring with
them the fabric of the past.

5. Understand the market - strategic decisions
must be made against a backdrop of market
intelligence. If your market is in decline you must
review your purpose in the light of these facts.
What skills do you have that could be used to
explore different market opportunities? If the skills
of your organisation can be leveraged to take
advantage of an emerging market, your new
sense of purpose and vision should reflect this.

6. Make sure the vision is understood by everyone
in the organisation - it is not enough to leave your
new sense of purpose just with the top team.
Getting everyone in the organisation
understanding and signed up to the vision is vital.

BACK to Basics

Similarly, when working inside an organisation, it can be difficult to get an objective overview - especially if it's in trouble. There are times when it might be helpful to hire an external view, but often a simple 'back to basics' session with your team can help. What you need is to gain a clear understanding of what's gone wrong and how to fix it. Successful businesses constantly review their core purpose in the light of market changes, opportunities and intuition. Getting the management team round the table at times like this is critical. Then what the business could and should be about can be discussed.

Overcoming Resistance

Senior teams can be uncomfortable going through these seemingly simplistic exercises. They are used to directing complex operational challenges, managing the scale implications of big budget and global reach. Sitting around a table discussing concepts and ideas can seem far removed and not relevant to their daily challenge. A good way to motivate leadership teams to create their vision is to assess the cost of not doing so. Put simply - do they want to:

- Ignore what their customers are saying
- Be blind to market trends
- Have a confused and de-motivated workforce
- Discount their heritage
- See their business fail

"Good business leaders create a vision, articulate the vision, passionately own the vision, and relentlessly drive it to completion."
Jack Welch

EXERCISE

How to Build a Mission Statement with a Team

*Objective: to create a mission statement by having the Team
frame their core purpose through breaking down their activities,
and describing them in the simplest terms. The aim is to be
clear, simple and accurate.*

1. Give each team member a stack of index cards.

2. Ask them to record key words only, that describe
the main purpose of the business

3. When they have finished ask them to place the
cards on a large tabletop – randomly.

4. Once all the cards are in place, ask the team to
cluster similar words.

5. Now ask them, individually to craft a core purpose
from this random word pattern onto an A4 sheet.

6. Post these on the wall when complete and
allow the team to read and acknowledge their
team members' contributions.

7. Now the individuals must work as a team to craft a
collective statement from their individual contributions.
This will result in a Vision or Mission statement.

EXAMPLE

Re-positioning a business

The Board of MailCo faced major challenges. The business had reached a level of maturity that was beginning to present a diminishing return. For the first time in its history, the business had delivered a negative profit. Costs were spiralling out of control and sales were showing a double-digit year on year decline. Originally the business had pioneered selling goods to people in their homes. Convenience for customers and commission for their sales agents were the key drivers of success. But times had changed. The launch of e-commerce and the emergence of large out of town retail outlets meant that the key business drivers were no longer appropriate or effective. The CEO and his senior team were facing a 're-invent or die' scenario. So they focused their attention on repositioning the strategic direction of the business.

It was vital to understand:

- What did their customers really want?
- Was it convenience, or new product and service offers?
- How able were they as a business to deliver this?
- Were their systems, offers, services and infrastructure geared up for this change in focus?
- Was commission-based agency selling out of line with today's world?
- What new possible markets and products might be available to them?

To build the strategic change plan, the team needed to understand where the business had come from. At an orientation session they considered the original business objectives alongside the changing market. Studying the economic, social and political climate enabled the team to see where the business was no longer meeting the needs of their customers. They compared their observations against customer research data. The result: they were able to form a clear view of what the business needed in order to get back in shape.

Mailco needed to reposition with a broader offer. One that could compete with the new market entrants based on a direct, rather than indirect sales model. This became new core purpose ['the what'] of Mailco's business, based on its historical and current key strengths, the marketplace and the wants and needs of its customers, existing and future. The Mailco team identified the key strengths and purpose of the business, and then synthesised some very complex strategic initiatives into one digestible statement. Mailco's Mission: 'To become the most accessible provider of products and services in the home shopping arena'.

Now, the challenge became how to communicate this new strategy in an easy to understand, compelling format that would touch the whole business. Avoiding a detailed process implementation plan, they focused attention on 'how things should be done round here' based on the core values of the organisation. What did they need to do to create ownership? They brainstormed the most important values that would support the company as well as themselves. Then they refined this list of values so that it would be reflected in all their core activities.

How to Get Buy-In

The CEO had previously observed the power of doing this Vision process in a former business. Because he was highly credible, it was possible for him to lead his group of fellow directors so they could keep an open mind and go with the process. Once the clarity started to build around their thinking, the team were more than happy to continue. Their buy-in to the process also supported the resulting communication of the mission statement throughout the rest of the business. Being clear about what it means if you don't do this exercise is the best way to sign up the top team.

"Vision is the blazing campfire around which people will gather. It provides light, energy, warmth and unity."
Bill Newman

Checklist: Test Your Mission Statement

☐   Does it describe your core purpose?

☐   Does it take into account the company's responsibilities to its stakeholders?

☐   Is the proposition attractive/ appealing?

☐   Does the statement promote the company's competitive advantage?

☐   Does it identify the values that link with the company's purpose?

☐   Can the company's people be proud of it?

☐   Do the values resonate with the company strategy?

☐   Is it easy to read and understand?

EXAMPLE

Promises: an Alternative Form of Vision Statement

Ian inherited some challenges when he took over a large region of a national branch network. Due to an outdated incentive system and an extremely poor internal communication system, sales needed a boost. The top team were in agreement that a traditional vision or mission statement would not be appropriate for their region. In fact, the organisation already had one in place. It worked for the group as a whole but didn't specifically address their challenges.

Thinking creatively, they decided to craft a series of promises that would connect their team in a positive way. The purpose of these promises was to show the wider network what was in it for them, as well as treating them with respect and honesty. This would help drive the sales line up and improve the way people communicated with each other. This simple promise approach translated easily to poster and leaflet format and helped get the network re-energised.

'Vision animates, inspires, transforms purpose into action.'
Warren Bennis

Here's what they promised:

Promise No 1:
We will get our resourcing right
What does it mean?
Having the right number of people, properly trained and in the
right jobs.

Promise No 2:
We will build a great team spirit of which we are all
incredibly proud
What does it mean?
Investing in our managers to enhance their leadership capability

Promise No 3:
We will deliver the best customer experience in the region
What does it mean?
Having great co-ordination in all our branches – getting major
premises issues sorted out quickly

Promise No 4:
We will listen to customers more than rivals
What does it mean?
Continually accessing the views of customers and giving them
feedback

Ian's team used the index card method (previously described) to create their promises, but their focus was their own regional activity. The company mission statement worked for the business as a whole but they wanted to specifically address their needs. The promises were generated in response to the core activities that were produced by the process. The index cards showed the need to have the right people, both in numbers and quality to satisfy and exceed customer expectation. Then the final crosscheck for the team was to ensure that their promises were congruent with the overall company mission statement.

"Leaders establish the vision for the future and set the strategy for getting there; they cause change. They motivate and inspire others to go in the right direction and they, along with everyone else, sacrifice to get there."
John Kotter

EXERCISE

Alignment with Your Values

If your values are out of alignment with your core purpose or vision, you will struggle to deliver your objective. If your heart isn't in something, it doesn't happen, or the result is less than satisfactory. Driving out core values and prioritising them can be achieved through the following simple process.

1. The team or individual begins by writing their own list of what values they hold important to them. If you are doing this in a group, record all the values on a flip chart. Once you have clustered and taken out duplication, post your people values on the wall.

2. Record in the same way the values of the organisation.

3. Post the two side by side on the wall and compare and contrast. There should be some similarities between the two. If you are not seeing this, your personal value sets are at odds with those of the organisation and this dissonance maybe causing problems for the business. The two need to align for best results.

Lists that are too long will not give you a clear set of values to compare. Simple lists work best to run your business. So it is essential to elicit the most important values. Ask the team/individual to measure every value against each other to determine relative importance and significance.

You will be left with the top priorities for you and the business in terms of 'how we do things round here'. This is your core value set. These can also be used to create a set of 'Promises' as an alternative to the more traditional mission statement.

EXERCISE

Evaluating your Values

Evaluate each digit on the top line against each digit on the bottom line to determine relative importance.

Your Values	Which is more important?

1 = Honesty

①1 1①
2③④5

*For Honesty, we can see that it is ranked **more** important than Creativity, but **less** important than Innovation, and so on.*

2 = Creativity

2 2 2
③④⑤

3 = Innovation

③③
4 5

4 = Respect

④
5

5 = Abundance

5

From these example rankings the three top values are:

> *Innovation (chosen 4 times)*
> *Respect (chosen 3 times)*
> *Honesty (chosen twice)*

EXERCISE

Check Stakeholder Congruence

How can you ensure that the mission statement you create is 'true' to the requirements of your key stakeholders? Your customers, shareholders as well as your people all need to be carefully considered when constructing a good Mission Statement or set of Promises.

Here is a quick and easy way to check the effectiveness and appropriateness of your new Vision:

1. Imagine the business is 5 years forward in time.

2. Ask your team to step into the shoes of each of your stakeholder groups, and to record on a flip chart what they will be saying about you when you have been successful.

3. Read back the reflections and check that the mission statement you have crafted as a team can deliver the stakeholder desire.

OWNERSHIP

Ownership of the Mission Statement

Once you are agreed on your mission it is helpful to 'seal the contract' with your team (and yourself). Now you have something tangible: the statement, your values and your promises, to sign up to. Physically signing your name to this and witnessing other's signatures, makes the process significant. Just like when you are buying a new home or getting married, adding your signature to the deal suddenly makes it real.

"A true leader is one who designs the cathedral and then shares the vision that inspires others to build it."
Jan Carlzon

COMMUNICATING the Vision

You may be a great leader with a great Vision for the business, but unless you can communicate it to the rest of the organisation, unless you can inspire people to deliver it, your great ideas will be ineffective. How can you effectively communicate the strategy of the business? It is not enough just to have a statement of your core purpose and direction; everybody must know what it is in order to deliver the promise. One of the most effective methods of strategic communication is the cascade principle. Starting with the leaders of the business, the message is cascaded through all levels of the organisation until each person is clear about where the business is headed.

No matter how large the organisation, this process will work. Maximum impact can be gained by using a combination of communication strategies. The more powerful the communication, the more inspired, 'bought-in' and connected are the people who are going to deliver. Each function or department of a business must own and sign-up to the top-level mission and core values of the organisation. They also need to fully understand their own part in that journey.

Leaders often find this communication a challenge because they assume that all areas of the business will be driven by the helicopter view similar to their own. In actual fact, what departments need is to understand their own strategic direction, and how it supports the overall vision. It's rather like a set of Russian dolls. Every piece fits well inside the other, but each

A man to carry on a successful business must have imagination.
He must see things in a vision, a dream of the whole thing.'
Charles M. Schwab

has its own individual flavour and feel. It is clear they all belong to the same family, they all fit but they also have their allowable differences. Once a leader or top team have acknowledged this, they can let go. Then they can allow the local interpretation, but be safe in the knowledge that the top-level vision will connect the whole organisation.

EXERCISE

Key Stages in the Cascade Process

How each department states their common purpose is a matter for local interpretation. Too many mission statements floating around a business can cause confusion. To create a functional Mission that sits well with the group vision, you can make use of 'Promises'. These provide clarity for specific departments but are also in total alignment with the company vision. When individuals understand how they uniquely support the organisation, they know how their role helps to deliver the mission. Like the story of the two men sweeping the floor at Cape Canaveral. When they were asked what they were doing, one said he was sweeping the floor, the other man said 'I'm helping to put a man on the moon.'

Stage One

'Tell' is the first stage of the communication. A well designed and crafted Mission Statement, Values and/or Promises are generated. The board or team need to be clear that this is a given. Consultation belongs at the 'build' stage of the vision rather then the communication stage. If debate is opened up during the cascade process it can lead to diffusion and confusion. Local interpretations can be managed at stage two of this process.

Stage Two

Each function or department needs to take their team through the same process as the board, to determine their own departmental core purpose that supports the top-level statement. If for example, the organisation's mission statement is:

'To provide customers with the most fashionable casual clothes at the best price in the market',

The buying department will need to align their purpose behind this. Their core purpose may be:

'To provide the fastest supply chain in the market place for high fashion goods'

Stage Three

A direct 'tell and share' approach is recommended for every new level of communication – backed up with visual reminders and documentation. Large conference formats and smaller awaydays are helpful to create this cascade. If a piece of music can be agreed on to represent the spirit of the organisation and its purpose this will help to anchor the message. Music is a very powerful anchor, which most people relate well to. If you are going to use this music publicly or in a published format you must observe the copyright laws.

The desired outcome of this cascade process is that every person in the business has heard, seen, has a copy of and can quote the core purpose of the business and their function's role in that vision.

"A true definition of an entrepreneur comes closer to:
A poet, visionary, or packager of social change."
Robert Schwartz

CHALLENGES for the Cascade

Challenges for the Cascade Process

Organisations/departments have different shapes. Some are **pointy** and have a few senior people who lead the business and many operational teams who support this pyramid structure. Others are **flat** with more senior and strategic people and few operators. The challenge to cascade strategic vision is far greater in pointy organisations. Highly operational structures often have vast numbers of individuals working shift patterns. Getting the messages to all people in a consistent and timely way is logistically challenging. **First class planning** is essential here to enable the organisation to get geared up together. In flatter organisations the messages can be fast and accurate.

Pointy Organisation

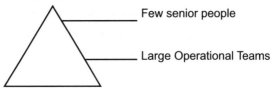

Few senior people

Large Operational Teams

Flat Organisation

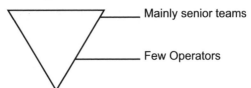

Mainly senior teams

Few Operators

A good example of a pointy department in a business would be customer service or logistics. Marketing departments are usually much flatter with very few operational staff. Before you start the cascade process it would be useful to determine: **What is the structure of your teams and departments?**

"Throughout the centuries there were men
who took first steps down new roads
armed with nothing but their own vision."
Ayn Rand

FEAR of Change

When Leaders start communicating their new Vision, their people hear 'change of direction'. Change, any kind of change, can feel challenging to some people. When your business is in trouble, you may need a change of direction, but that's when you most need to take account of some of the negative impacts of change. It is advisable to seek change management expertise to support you through the early stages of implementation. If you can manage the fear of change effectively, you are far more likely to succeed. Change makes people uncomfortable. You may need to address this fear of change if you notice the following symptoms:

- Uncertainty
- Confusion
- The need to think
- The need for energy
- The fear of failure
- The fear of diminishing past success

Any cascade communication process needs to address these issues. When businesses begin to implement their vision, they often don't have all the answers but a simple Q&A sheet can at least acknowledge some of the things people will be feeling in a very uncertain climate.

EXERCISE

Good questions for leaders to ask themselves at this point:

Q. What will we preserve/what will stay the same?

Q. What will we stop doing because it's never served us well?

Q. What will we stop doing because it's time to move on?

Q. What will we start doing?

Sample FAQs: Have Your Answers Ready

It's also a good idea to be prepared to answer the questions that may arise about proposed changes of direction.

Q. Will there be job losses as a result of this change?

A. It's difficult to tell at this point in time but we will keep you fully informed.

Q. Why can't we carry on as before, why do we have to change?

A. If we don't do something different the business will not survive. We are not making any profit and our sales are in decline. We know that we have the skills in the business to survive and we think that the new strategy will bring future success.

Q. What will this mean for me?

A. Respecting people and being honest are key to our future success and we are going to discuss what it will mean for us.

Q. What happens if we don't succeed?

A. We believe that we can based on what we know about our market, our products and services and, most importantly, our people.

TIME Constraints

Getting the new Vision message cascaded quickly is vital in order to get the business moving. If the business is in trouble, speed is even more essential! The cascade process can seem very heavy on time and slow to produce results. But the cost of not doing it is far higher. People maybe doing things quickly but will they know why? Will they be doing the right things to deliver it?

To speed up the process, block out time for it to happen. Make it clear that this is not just another thing for managers to do. Mark it out as THE MOST IMPORTANT thing.

The mistake many teams make is to spend the greater proportion of their time creating the Vision. In fact, the major time and effort should be focussed on communicating it and delivery. It is really not enough to have a mission statement or a vision, **people must know what it is, what it means and how they are going to deliver it.**

CORPORATE Jargon

Jargon is the curse of the modern business. 'Management speak' creates confusion and distance. In very big organisations, with a wide mix of levels and functional cultures, sometimes each department will have its own different 'language'. So, when planning your communication use simple language that everyone will understand. If you have used the simple methodology to build your vision, don't destroy the clarity by using phrases that the majority of the business won't understand (or worse may despise). Try to avoid phrases like:

Going forward	*In the Target*
Landing the Message	*Adding texture*
Bandwidth	*Emotional leakage*
In Scope	*Helicopter View*
Blue Sky	*On Board*

These are phrases that are used by managers to denote membership of the leadership club but they will alienate the wider team. Thankfully there is currently a trend towards simplicity and hopefully this will manifest itself with less business speak.

Some very large organisations do have their own language that everybody in the business understands. This is quite rare and it shows the organisation is first-class at cascading information. When a business has its own phraseology though, care must be taken if the Mission Statement will be made public. It needs to be understood by the wider community too.

> *"It is a mistake to look too far ahead.*
> *Only one link in the chain of destiny can be handled at a time."*
> Winston Churchill

7 Keys to Successful Cascading

1. The first stage of the process must be 'tell'
– consultation can lead to diffusion and confusion

2. Each department must interpret how they can
support the vision/mission – build their own core
purpose and values. If their values are out of
alignment with the top level set – cultural
differences may exist which may be a challenge
– the further away they are, the less effective will
be their support of the business

3. The information must be communicated to
everybody in the business. Useful methods
for getting this reach are conferences, functional
meetings, intranet, notice boards, and team
meetings, launch events and social areas.

4. Check that the message has been 'heard'
– feedback is essential. Create mechanisms that
are simple so you get maximum response.

5. Don't just rely on bits of paper. Talking is
essential. Unless people hear the message the
seeing will not have the same impact.

6. Use simple language

7. Understand and acknowledge the negative as
well as the positive impact of change

KEEPING the Message Alive

Bits of paper and words, however exciting at the time, can soon fade from the memory. One way to keep the message alive is to **translate it onto a 'keep-able' format**. Laminators are really useful for taking messages and turning them into credit card-sized reminders. Mouse mats and screen savers are also useful ways of keeping the message front of mind. Organisations sometimes make the mistake of flooding the workplace with bits of paper that end up yellowing on notice boards or languishing in in-trays. Make your reminders tangible and practical.

REGULAR Scoring of the Vision

Re-visiting the mission/vision and values at regular intervals is essential. Markets change, opportunities present themselves and skills sets evolve.What was true two years ago, may not be true today. With technology moving at the pace we see today, no business can afford to be complacent about their core purpose. Building core purpose review sessions into the strategic process will ensure that your vision is current and worthwhile.You can also build the vision and values into the scorecard of the business where they will be constantly visible and checked against the key measures of the business

A typical business scorecard would look at the four quadrants of people, customer, process and revenue/sales/profit. By having the vision central to the scorecard, it will always provide a focus, which supports the whole.

Balanced Business Scorecard integrating Vision

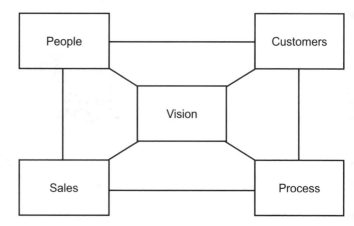

CLIMATE Surveys

Climate surveys provide a litmus reading of the culture and clarity of the business. They tell leaders:

- How happy and motivated the workforce are
- If the business is doing things the right way
- If the business is doing the right things
- If the leadership is doing its job well
- If communication processes are robust
- If people like what they do and understand why they are doing it.

Such climate surveys should always include a check on the understanding and awareness of the vision. If you are getting consistently low awareness or misunderstanding, you will need to refresh your cascade process. Functional meetings (or town hall meetings as they are commonly referred to), are good for this type of exercise. You can communicate with large groups of people in a very informal way. Questions from the floor, gathered during the session, are a great way to clear up confusion and an opportunity for who ever is holding the meeting to re-affirm the '**What**' and the '**How**'.

REFRESH your Mission Statement

Refresh Your Mission Statement - Treat as an Iterative Process

Refreshing your mission is as important as creating one in the first place. At least every couple of years, make sure you check the relevance of your core purpose against the new climate: economic, social and cultural. It will be particularly important to check congruence with your stakeholders and to check that your core value sets are still in alignment with your business direction.

"Without vision the people perish."
Bible: Proverbs 29:18

VISION: the Vital Way Forward

Whether the business is big or small, you need to understand where you are going. Whether the quest is driven by start-up, crisis, innovation or growth, getting down to basics is the way to clarify the true Vision. Being clear about the 'What' as well as the 'How' is vital before you can even begin to think about a Mission Statement. What is this company about, what are its strengths, what are the products? How does this company deliver those? Enlist the cooperation and support of your management team. When their values are congruent with the values of the company, then it will be easy to brainstorm the perfect words for a Mission Statement. But then the question is how to facilitate passion, energy and consistent delivery of the Vision? Building a Vision is the easy part, cascading the message throughout the organisation requires time, effort, planning and dedication. The importance of keeping the Vision alive, in front of everyone's mind, must be clearly understood. All your business measures must incorporate the Vision consistently. You need to minimise the impact of change and focus on the positive, tangible results of working together as one unified team. A good Vision can transform the business.

'A vivid image compels the whole body to follow.'
Aristotle

About the
CONTRIBUTORS

ARIELLE Essex

Arielle specialises in grooming executives for career advancement, enhancing communication, increasing credibility and gravitas, improving state management, as well as gracefully handling strategic political situations. Certified in Charisma and Group Leadership Dynamics, she combines a powerful range of skills to coach people for excellence. Some of this work includes immediate video and computer bio-feedback for maximum value.

Originally from the USA, Arielle has navigated her own career through four different industries starting with Advertising, Illustration, Design & Copywriting; then complementary medicine working as an Osteopath, Naturopath & Kinesiologist. Later, this evolved into studying Psychology, NLP, EFT, HeartMath and Emotional Intelligence. She became a certified NLP Master Practitioner and Trainer, set up her own training business in 1995 (www.PracticalMiracles.com). She is a certified Coach with Erickson College (accredited with ICF), Her first book was published in 2004, *'Compassionate Coaching'*.

Arielle loves helping Leaders achieve their potential and understand the dynamics that support change both personally, in groups and throughout an organisation.

ROSE Padfield

Rose began her career more than twenty years ago, and has worked across many sectors and geographies, supporting business and its leaders. Much of this has been in environments in the midst of significant change with no clear boundaries, and influencing and motivating others becomes a significant challenge. With a Masters degree in Strategic HR, with a focus on change management, she has used this learning to practical effect within large, global corporations.

Having seen the value in creating focused time for these leaders to examine and improve their style and performance, she decided to set up her own business. Through coaching teams and individuals across Europe, Rose has helped many people to gain more fulfilment in their working and personal lives. Having coached leaders to see the impact they have on themselves and others, the knock-on effect from individual to company level shows a significant ROI for the time investment.

Seeing an individual move from a place of uncertainty and stress, to one where they have high self esteem, personal power, and influence is why Rose loves her work!

TANYA Yazdanpanahi

Tanya Yazdanpanahi began her career consulting in the field of Occupational Psychology after attaining her Masters where she specialised in Stress Management. She progressed to working in-house for a number of blue chip organisations across both the IT and Financial Services sectors where she held a number of senior leadership positions. As a result of her diverse experience, she brings solutions to businesses and individuals that are grounded in organisational development best practice but tailored to their context, commercial situations and cultures.

She left corporate life in 2001 to set up her own business and focus full time on her passion to help people and teams change to realise their true potential. Her insights and inherent ability to make connections and see the bigger picture combined with her practical, realistic and honest approach enables her clients to achieve and sustain high performance and be at their best more of the time.

LIZ Hunt

Liz Hunt has nearly fifteen years experience working nationally and internationally developing leaders to manage themselves and their teams during periods of change. Originally starting life in IT revolutionising the way people worked she now specialises in working with organisations and leaders to identify and remove barriers to business success, creates constructive working relationships thus increasing contribution.

Major successes have included:

- Revitalising a division where morale was "on the floor" to enabling the leadership team to inspire and motivate themselves and staff. The impact was that they not only maintained their results, but 'smashed them' showing a direct ROI (sometimes results dip when leaders focus on internal matters).
- Bringing leadership teams together in merger situations and re-engaging managers who felt they were no-longer at the top table!

When a new team is urgently required to fulfil priority objectives, Liz takes the strain out of this often hit-and-miss task!

Liz believes that "as change is more common in people's lives they need to learn skills to be clear on what they and their organizations need at that time, to adapt, refocus and re-communicate changes effectively to reduce wasted time and energy. These aren't nice to have skills they are essential business capabilities. It needs to become second nature at every level."

Being clear on what's important to you is essential to balancing your life and negotiating what you want.

She holds a Masters in Management Learning specialising in Cultural Change, is an international NLP trainer and is a qualified Master NLP practitioner. She has her own business and has led workshops and seminars on leadership, time management, facilitation and presentation skills, on customer relations management, stress management, team development and much more.

MAGGIE Rose

Maggie Rose started her career in the retail and services sector. A breadth of business experience gathered over 20 years in stores, commercial, operational management and HR from the shop floor to the Board room, led her to build the foundations of MROI in 1993.

Maggie noticed a dissatisfaction with the level of return organisations achieved when investing in people initiatives. From identifying what was missing, she created a new way of working with clients that accelerates achievement of business results, by increasing contribution from both individuals and teams at senior levels. She personally gains most fulfilment from working with leaders who want to elevate the contribution they make through the privilege and power of their role.

Throughout Asia, US, and Europe she has delivered over 10,000 hours of individual coaching with senior leaders. Her intuition and creativity combined with her pragmatic approach and business experience offer a challenging and dynamic style as a business leader, consultant and coach.

Maggie says: "I believe that commercial organisations have a powerful presence in this world. Way beyond countries. Way beyond governments. The opportunity for leaders in organisations is to choose how they want to use that power – for themselves, their organisation and the world. What excites me about my work is the increasingly greater contribution that those individual leaders and organisations can make and choose to make."

CHRISTINE Southam

Christine Southam chose to leave her main board position with an International retailer to pursue a career in the field of personal development. With first hand experience of running a large, commercial organisation with a turnover in excess of £1 billion, she is well placed to coach top talent in all aspects of career and personal development.

Chris has held senior positions in Marketing and HR. Her focus is on 'self-marketing' and personal branding. She has clients in both the corporate and private sector, specialising in helping people identify and achieve the next stage in their career.

She embraces a wide range of creative tools and techniques to deliver action-oriented solutions. Chris combines this approach with her Board experience and commercial knowledge, to support individuals and teams in the focus and delivery of their goals. Her commercial experience ensures both credibility and empathy with the senior leaders that she works with in business.

Chris is also an award-winning image consultant and Master of the Federation of Image Consultants. She has helped many senior people in business define and refine their executive presence. She works with clients to help them present their personal 'brand'. Clients from many walks of life, including politics and light entertainment have benefited from Chris' support.

Having begun her career in Marketing as a copywriter she has always enjoyed the power of the written word and understands the benefit of a clear, simple approach to get the message across. Chris is often asked to speak to large organisations about the work that she does and she delivers development workshops all over the world.

Her passion in life is to facilitate individuals in the achievement of excellence and potential in both their business and personal lives. She is a graduate of Warwick University and holds postgraduate qualifications from the University of London. Chris is a fully qualified NLP practitioner and graduate of one of Europe's leading coaching academies.

Further Reading

REFERENCES

John Baldoni, *Great Communication Secrets of Great Leaders* (McGraw-Hill, 2003) ISBN 0 07 141496 7

Jack Black, *Mindstore for Personal Development* (Thorsons,1996) ISBN 0 7225 3350 0

Business Communication, *Harvard Business Essentials* (HBS Press, 2003) ISBN 1 59139 113 X

Craig Chappelow and Jean Brittain Leslie, *Throwing the right switches: How to keep your executive career on track* from *The CCL Guide to Leadership in Action* edited by Martin Wilcox and Stephen Rush (John Wiley and Sons, 2004) ISBN 978 0 787 97370 4

Shelle Rose Charvet, *Words that Change Minds: Mastering the Language of Influence* (Kendall Hunt Pub Co, 1997) ISBN 978 0 787 23479 9

Robert Cialdini, *Influence, the Psychology of Persuasion* (Quill, 1993) ISBN 0 688 128 16 5

Jim Collins, *Good to Great: Why Some Companies Make the Leap...and Others Don't* (HarperCollins, 2001) ISBN 0 06 662099 6

Steven Covey, *7 Habits of Highly Effective People* (Simon & Schuster, 1990) ISBN 0 671 70863 5

Steven Covey, *First Things First* (Simon & Schuster, 1995)
ISBN 0 684 80203 1

Gordon Dryden and Jeannette Vos, *The Learning Revolution*
(The Learning Web, 1999) ISBN 1 880396 66 1

Arielle Essex, *Compassionate Coaching: How to Heal Your Life
and Make Miracles Happen* (Rider & Co, 2004) ISBN 1 8441
3236 6

Daniel Goleman, *Emotional Intelligence; why it can matter more
than IQ (*Bantam Books, 1995) ISBN 0 553 09503 X

Goleman, D, Boyatzis, R & Mckee, A, *The New Leaders;
Transforming the Art of Leadership into the Science of Results*
(Little, Brown, Great Britain, 2002) ISBN 0-316-85766-1 (In the
USA, this book is published by the Harvard Business School
Press 2002 as *Primal Leadership*)

John Gray, *Men are from Mars Women are from Venus*
(Thorsons, 1993) ISBN 0 7225 2840 X

Michael Grinder, *Charisma – The Art of Relationships* (Michael
Grinder & Associates, 2004) ISBN 1 883407 10 9

Michael Grinder, *The Elusive Obvious: The Science of Non-
Verbal Communication* (Michael Grinder & Associates, 2007)
ISBN 978 1 883 40713 1

Barbara Hemphill, *Taming the Paper Tiger at Work* (Kiplinger Washington Editors Inc.) ISBN 0 938721 58 5

JCA (Occupational Psychologists), founded 2003
www.jca.biz

Sue Knight, *NLP at Work: The Difference that Makes a Difference in Business* (Nicholas Brealey Publishing, 1995) ISBN 1 85788 070 6

Sue Knight, *NLP Solutions: How to Model What Works in Business to Make it Work for You* (Nicholas Brealey Publishing, 1999) ISBN 1 85788 227 X

Genie Z Laborde, *Influencing with Integrity: Management Skills for Communication and Negotiation* (Crown House Publishing, 1984) ISBN 1 89983 601 2

Joseph O' Connor, *NLP Workbook: A Practical Guide to Achieving the Results You Want* (Thorsons, 2001) ISBN 0 00 710003 5

Richard Pound, *Crucial Conversations, Tools for Talking When Stakes are High* (McGraw-Hill, 2008) ISBN 978 0 07 148499 2

David Richo, *How to be an Adult* (Paulist Press, 1991) ISBN 0 809 13223 0

Marshall B Rosenberg PhD, *Non-Violent Communication: A Language Of Life* (PuddleDancer Press, 2003) ISBN 1 892005 02 6

Susan Scott, *Fierce Conversations: Achieving Success at Work & in Life, One Conversation at a Time* (Berkley Books, 2004) ISBN 0 425 19337 3

Steven J Stein PhD & Howard E Book MD, *The EQ Edge: Emotional Intelligence and Your Success (*Jossey-Bass, 2006) ISBN 978 0 470 83836 5

Sun Tzu, *The Art Of War* (Multiple sources and translations, please see http://en.wikipedia.org/wiki/The_Art_of_War)

The examples used throughout this book have been altered to preserve anonymity but permission has been sought and granted to reproduce them if required.

CONTACT us

MROI
PO Box 943
Guildford
GU1 9AB

www.mroi.com